BRAVING DIFFICULT DECISIONS

BRAVING DIFFICULT DECISIONS

What to Do When You Don't Know What to Do

*

ANGELA WILLIAMS GORRELL

WILLIAM B. EERDMANS PUBLISHING COMPANY
GRAND RAPIDS, MICHIGAN

Wm. B. Eerdmans Publishing Co.
2006 44th Street SE, Grand Rapids, MI 49508
www.eerdmans.com

Book design by Lydia Hall

Printed in the United States of America

31 30 29 28 27 26 25   1 2 3 4 5 6 7

ISBN 978-0-8028-8397-1

Library of Congress Cataloging-in-Publication Data

A catalog record for this book is available from the Library of
Congress.

The untitled poem by Joy Sullivan quoted at the beginning of chapter 6
is printed with permission.

For my younger sister, Jenna.
You are wiser and braver than you know.

I feel so lucky that we are not just sisters, but best friends.
Thank you for always having my back.

To you and your family, Rob, Andi, and Ro,
thanks for being a second home for me.
On those days I needed it most.
And on every other kind of day.

CONTENTS

Contents

HOW TO READ THIS BOOK

Life is full of hard decisions, and this book is designed to be a sturdy and trusted resource you can return to again and again. Each time your questions are likely to be a bit different. So here are three ways you can engage this material based on your particular needs at any given crossroads.

- Set off on a journey. Begin with chapter 1 and follow the chapters like a road map that starts at "Stirring" and leads you step-by-step toward a decision. After reading each chapter, do the corresponding exercise in the appendix.
- Begin with prayer. Each chapter in this book is animated by a question and related prayer. You'll find these couplets throughout the book, but they're also collected on page x. Review the list and read the chapter animated by the prayer that resonates most deeply with you in this moment. Follow that chapter with the related exercise in the appendix.
- First take stock. The appendix is chock-full of exercises that help you apply each chapter to your own life. These exercises can also help clarify your goals at the outset of reading this book. For example, chapter 1's iceberg exercise can help you get clear on the different aspects of your difficult decision. Review the appendix and select an exercise or two that helps you first do some essential inner work that will support you on this journey.

QUESTIONS AND PRAYERS

CHAPTER 1: STIRRING
Question: What is happening?
Prayer: Help me.

CHAPTER 2: SURRENDERING
Question: Where do I start?
Prayer: Be with me.

CHAPTER 3: SEEKING
Question: Who should I ask for advice?
Prayer: Speak to me.

CHAPTER 4: SENSING
Question: How do I deal with my feelings?
Prayer: Steady me.

CHAPTER 5: SUMMONING
Question: Who am I?
Prayer: Inspire me.

CHAPTER 6: SHEDDING
Question: Why can't I move forward?
Prayer: Relieve me.

CHAPTER 7: SIFTING
Question: How do I know what is true?
Prayer: Teach me.

CHAPTER 8: SELECTING
Question: What is mine to do?
Prayer: Enlighten me.

CHAPTER 9: SEARCHING
Question: What am I being led to do?
Prayer: Show me.

CHAPTER 10: STRIVING
Question: What if?
Prayer: Encourage me.

CHAPTER 11: SATED JOY
Question: How do I live into my story?
Prayer: Thank you.

WHY AND HOW I WROTE THIS BOOK

This book contains two journeys: mine and yours.

Several years ago, I hit a wall. I had invested much of my life in relationships and institutions that were crumbling. And my own sense of self and purpose was crumbling along with them. As I was trying to figure out what to do in my own life, I read some wonderful books on decision making and discernment. But the spiritual books were not always very practical, and the practical books often did not account for the reader's spiritual life. I needed both. And I needed more.

I needed a book that could journey with me into my personal thicket of fear, shame, hope, and faith, and guide me back out again. And as an avid people pleaser, I was especially eager to know what to do if my decisions disappointed other people.

I soon learned I wasn't alone. As I reached out to people in person and online about their hardest decisions, I heard many persistent, familiar questions.

"What if I made a bad decision recently and can't trust myself anymore?"

"What do I do when I feel powerless?"

"How do I deal with difficult feelings?"

"Who do I listen to?"

In these conversations I learned a great deal about what makes difficult decisions difficult. And I decided I wanted to write a book that would speak to both personal and universal dimensions of each scenario people shared with me.

To this end, I have braided together three major strands of research to create the journey this book invites you on: (1) various discernment processes and methods for making decisions, (2) the stories of historical figures who made challenging choices, and (3) interviews with people who have recently made hard decisions.

First, there are many books about decision making from a wide variety of perspectives—some more helpful than others, few of them presenting the breadth of wisdom I sought. So, I've gleaned what I believed to be the best guidance from this literature to offer a holistic approach to discernment that is both practical *and* spiritual.

Second, I read the biographies and autobiographies of people who have made difficult decisions, some widely known like Jackie Robinson, others less known like Amma Syncletica. What these people have in common is an incredible capacity to make bold choices, even when it did not benefit them directly, even when their very lives or life as they knew it was at stake. I wondered, how did they figure out what to do? How did they become wise? What kind of people did they need to become to be able to boldly make their choice?

Third, I also interviewed people who have made all sorts of difficult decisions in our contemporary context. I talked to Jesse, who stayed married after several difficult years of separation, and Gen, who divorced after twenty years of abuse. I talked with William, who chose not to die by suicide and instead to tackle an addiction that had a hold on his life. I learned from Marcus, who took a break from graduate school to focus on his mental health.

I interviewed Roseline, who pursued her deepest passion with a lot of uncertainty; Carol, who retired from a job she loved; and Lydia, who quit a "dream job" she thought she would love after ten months. I also talked with people who started businesses, left churches after attending them for years, ended relationships, and were willing to be arrested for something they believed in. From these conversations, I gained insight into the different ways people get clarity on what they should do. The stories of several people that I interviewed are in this book. Some chose to use their real first name, and others chose a pseudonym.

I pulled together habits of wisdom from these three strands of research to create ways of moving forward that resonate with our deepest values and God-breathed desires. Each year we get to live requires us to make new decisions, many of them difficult. And I hope this book becomes a trusted guide you can return to throughout your life, a sturdy and flexible resource that doesn't pretend to know what you should do but offers you ways to figure out where God is leading you. A book about *how* to make wise decisions, not what decisions to make.

I come to you as a human who has journeyed through heart-wrenching decisions several times, and I include my experiences throughout the book, too. You are not alone! Let's begin.

PROLOGUE

If you are feeling unsettled, unfulfilled, or undone, welcome. If you are at a crossroads or have experienced crisis and you need guidance, this book is for you. If you are in the liminal space between not knowing what to do and doing something meaningful, you are not alone. If you have a big decision, choice, change, or transition to make or a question to answer, and you are wondering how you are going to figure this out, help is at hand.

You may be trying to figure out what to do for work or about a dysfunctional work environment or what to do during retirement. Perhaps you feel burned out or are experiencing what some might call a midlife crisis. (I prefer midlife revival.) Maybe you do not know what college to attend or whether to make a move or become a parent. Perhaps you have recently experienced a devastating event and you know change is coming—within you, in your circumstances, or both—and you are trying to discern what to do in the midst of that change. Maybe you have been diagnosed with a chronic or terminal illness and you are wondering what the next right thing is. You may be struggling with a looming decision about a relationship. Perhaps inertia has you stuck and you are wondering how to live more meaningfully. Maybe your life feels chaotic and you need an exit ramp that is neither avoidance nor self-medication.

You might be asking any number of questions: Should I stay or should I go? Should I define the relationship, get married, break up, get divorced? Should I start this thing, quit this thing? Should I change careers? Should I leave this group, join this group? Should I say yes or no? What should I do next? What am I being called to do now? Your questions might be more expansive: Who am I? How can I feel more alive?

I hope every chapter of this book feels like you have met with someone over coffee or tea who has held space with you and given you a next step in your journey. No one can take this journey for you. No one but you can make your decision, change, choice, or transition, or answer the questions you have. But this book can be your companion. If you engage wholeheartedly in this journey, you will feel more capable and courageous. You will gain clarity about the situation you find yourself in. You will create space in your life to reflect, to take a deep breath, to truly attend to the voice of God, and to discern what to do.

You *are* being led, not just by the wisdom of the stories others have lived, but by the God who made the sun and the moon and the stars. You are not forgotten. You may feel lonely. I get that, trust me. But you're not alone.

I wrote this book after making two wildly difficult decisions within a two-year period.

I got divorced.

I work in the fields of theology and spirituality, which made my decision even more difficult. It was truly and without a doubt the most gut-wrenching decision I have ever made.

The most important thing I have learned as a divorced person is that no one ever anticipates getting a divorce and no one gets a divorce without experiencing suffering—whether during the marriage, during the divorce, long afterward, or at all three times. But this book does not talk about my marriage. Rather, I share my discernment process that led to me making my decision to get divorced and how I navigated the choppy waters in its wake.

My goal is not that you reach the same decisions as me or the other people featured in this book, but that you learn how to take your own journey into and through difficult decisions.

I also left a very stable job.

It was a unicorn-type job, the one job everyone in my field was supposed to want. I was a tenure-track professor at an "R1" university (a fancy way of saying a university that prioritizes research and respect for scholarship) and had just been approved to go up for tenure. Academia is an increasingly precarious profession, and tenure ostensibly provides enduring stability and respect from colleagues. I was on the cusp of achieving this brass ring of academic life, assured by my department it was a lock.

And then I left. Why? Because God told me God had something different for me, a more healthy and more meaningful life than what was available to me at that time. But the eight months that I spent trying to figure out what to do were not easy. The journey in this book helped me to figure out what to do.

It is my great hope that you will find your own story in between the lines of this book. If you let it, I believe this book and the invitations and stories within it will create space in your life for you to feel your own heartbeat and to hear the sound of the God who made your heartbeat.

Each chapter has a guiding question that people ask when they are trying to figure out what to do as well as a simple prayer that you can cling to throughout this journey. That is what this book is, a journey. It is your companion as you make a decision, a change, as you evolve.

The simplicity of the prayers throughout this book belies their power. Even if you do not know if God is listening, feel free to whisper, scream, or silently breathe out these prayers along your own journey.

If you are struggling with a decision or a looming transition, you are likely feeling afraid, fragile, worried, and overwhelmed. You may feel terrified by the mere idea of "different." Often when we have a big decision or change to make, we get consumed by the prospects of doing the wrong thing, messing up our life, and not finding the life we were meant to live. The "what-ifs" devour our curiosity and imagination. What if I make the wrong decision? What if people do not support me? What if I hurt even more? What if I regret what I do?

It is very easy to get lost in a perpetual state of analysis paralysis.

This book is a journey where you take one step at a time and as you move, you lean more and more into trusting God, yourself, and the process. This book is going to help you to engage your life and questions with more interest, wonder, and creativity, with less fear and anxiety.

A gentle reminder: You have not done anything life altering yet, and simply thinking about change does not make it happen, so take a deep breath. Lay down your worry for now. I promise you can always pick it back up! But for now, I encourage you to put down worry and pick up curiosity.

Maybe by the end of this book, your decision will be "not yet." Maybe you will make a more subtle change within, rather than a significant change in your circumstances.

The journey is just as important as any shift, decision, or choice you make. The journey itself will help you to feel more seen, more connected, more at peace.

And if you are pretty certain you need to make a change but feel stuck—too old, too young, too boxed in, too far gone, too inexperienced, too nervous, too unsupported, too scared, too unimportant, too locked in, too anything—I have news for you.

You can edit the story you are living.

I spent the first eighteen years of my life in Kentucky, first in Appalachia, and then in central Kentucky. I have lived in Oklahoma, Connecticut, Texas, and California, specifically Los Angeles, twice. So I have spent significant time across the United States. I was mostly raised middle class, save for a few difficult years after my parents got divorced. As an adult, I have lived both paycheck to paycheck and with a very comfortable amount of money coming in.

I am writing this book as I enter a new decade, my forties. I do so with gratitude for my ancestors; for my living family members, friends, and colleagues; and for a world that has often left me spellbound by its mysteries.

My background is Western and Christian. Thanks to an Ancestry DNA test, I know I primarily have Scottish, English, Norwegian, and

Welsh roots. I grew up in church and am an ordained minister in the Mennonite tradition, but between multiple deaths in my family over the last six years, divorce, moves, and the pandemic, I am struggling to figure out which Christian community is a good fit. At the end of the day, I sense God's presence in the world, and sometimes in my own daily life. I have been in awe on numerous occasions of God's outrageous miracles and goodness.

I hope you will feel welcomed by me and the journey of this book even if my background is not like yours at all and even if you don't feel connected to Christianity. I am sharing a bit of my story, recognizing that what I have experienced shapes how I think about making difficult decisions, shifts, and change. Perhaps take some time now to think about your story of origin and how who you are shapes the way you think about hard choices, transitions, and transformation.

Sometimes just realizing how we have been shaped provides clarity. For example, "Oh, of course I am terrified by the idea of moving. I had to move when I was seven after my parents divorced, and it was hard to make new friends." Or, "Interesting, I grew up in a family where everyone had a role and we were supposed to stick to it and now that I am considering this change, I am anxious about rocking the boat."

Before we set off on our journey, I invite you to take some time to consider where you start from. How did you grow up? What stage of your life are you in now? And how are all of these things colliding with the question you have, the looming decision you need to make, or the transition that is coming? Perhaps offer yourself some grace for feeling the way you do. It is all right to be in the liminal space between not knowing what to do and doing something meaningful.

As you read, I hope you will continue to offer yourself the compassion and space you need to take a wise next step.

Chapter 1 invites you to reflect on what is stirring within you. It is an invitation for you to go on a journey to figure out what to do. In chapter 2, you will read about what surrender looks like and feels like, and you will be given insight into why surrender is the mysterious but incredibly powerful first step in your journey.

Chapter 3 will help you to figure out who to invite on this journey with you. And in chapter 4, you will find practical ways to constructively express difficult emotions.

Chapter 5 will help you imagine the future by drawing on the stories that have made you, while chapter 6 will help you to let go of anything that is holding you back from moving forward in your life.

In chapters 7 and 8, you will receive guidance on discerning how your convictions and values inform your decision-making process.

Chapter 9 is about how to think critically and theologically about the different paths and possibilities you could pursue. Chapter 10 will help you to anticipate and plan for challenging conversations and give you the courage to make your decision, even if it involves risk.

Chapter 11 helps you to live toward your decision wholeheartedly. This chapter focuses on gratitude for the journey and finding contentment in your emerging story.

Throughout the book, you will hear compelling stories of others—impactful historical figures, Bible characters, and living, everyday people who have engaged in the steps of this journey and also made difficult decisions, transitions, and change. The stories of others will inspire and help you.

By the end of the book, if you give yourself over to this journey, you will have named possibilities and pathways and made a decision or change. And maybe, just maybe, sated joy will find you along the way.

If you are reading this book still breathing, your story is still being written. This is beautiful news. And you are worthy of this journey.

STIRRING

When You Don't Know What to Do

Some things break our hearts but fix our vision.

—Billie Eidson

For as long as you can remember, the faucet has been on. You have been pouring yourself out—into work, school, family, friends, organizations, community. Even on days you were exhausted, the water flowed. You were often stressed, but it seemed like the water would never run out. You could always squeeze out one more sentence, make one more try, pencil one more thing onto the calendar, give one more impression that you're satisfied.

Look, I am at this event! Look, my family is together! Look, I have friends! Look at my accomplishment! Look at the food I'm eating! Look at the thing I just bought! Look, I've lost five pounds (again)! Look at me on vacation! Look at my Christmas photo! Look, I made it here with clothes on! All is well!

But the other day, in a singular moment, the faucet turned off. The steady stream of energy and motivation that had always been there was suddenly gone.

Perhaps you feel you have lost yourself. How can this be? You're right here. Yet you look into the mirror and don't recognize the face that stares back at you. You have been cracked open, and like an egg, you're so all over the place that putting yourself back together again in the same way is impossible.

Something has to change.

> *Question: What is happening?*
> *Prayer: Help me.*

Your time is up.

You must decide whether to stay or go, whether to follow through with the project or let it die, whether to get married or break up.

It is time to have the conversation or to make a plan.

Perhaps you have nearly received the degree and it is time to figure out what is next.

Maybe you're midway through life, and unexpectedly it dawns on you that you're as close to needing a ride to a friend's house as you are to needing a knee replacement and you're wondering how to spend the next years of your life. Perhaps you are almost to the stage of life when you can't biologically have kids or even adopt, so you need to decide.

Or in your case, all of your kids have moved out and moved on. You have to figure out what to do between 5:00 and 9:00 p.m., how to relax, how to cook for fewer people, what you even like to do for fun.

Perhaps your parents need more care, and you're trying to figure out what to do to help them.

Or maybe your body can't do the thing it has loved for years—that sport, that hobby, that job. Possibly, you have reached the age when you must retire from your organization or the thing you have loved all your life.

Maybe in your case, you still have a lot of years ahead of you, and you're wondering, Did I already live the greatest year of my life?

Is there life after being an athlete, a musician, an actor, a dancer . . . is there life beyond this incredible thing I have done and can't do anymore? Whatever it is—a necessary transition, a new season, a breaking point, adulthood, midlife, menopause, retirement, end of life—the time has come. *You are at a crossroads.*

*

You're conflicted.

You are constantly trying to remember those first few weeks, that time when you felt wildly over the moon about that other person, and they you. When they kissed you, the whole world faded and you didn't care. Their eyes told you they loved you, even if they had not said it yet. But now, you try to avoid their gaze. It's too confusing or too painful.

You can't remember the last time you truly enjoyed one another's company. You fight so much that you also can't remember the last time you had a civil dialogue. You're wondering how long you can put up with this. You feel misunderstood, neglected, invisible. Their words and actions (and often even more so their lack of words and inaction) have you feeling profoundly lonely. There is nothing worse than feeling alone in a crowded room.

Maybe you feel next to nothing: passionless. Your conversations are vanilla. You're bored and it frightens you. You're tired of trying to make this work, of pretending like everything is okay.

You scan photos from the past hoping to find some secret buried in them about how to go back to the way things used to be when you laughed more than you cried.

You fill your life with as much as possible so you don't have to make a conversation or, worse, make love. To do so is like trying to connect with concrete—hard, unbending, cold.

There is a chasm between you two now, and you don't have the resources to navigate it. They have changed. You have changed.

It is also possible that a different kind of relationship is weighing on you—one with a friend or family member. You are wondering whether to let them go, forgive, create boundaries, speak up, invite transformation, or seek to repair it.

No matter what you are dealing with, something has to give. *You care about this person, and the relationship needs to be different.*

*

You're treading water.

Your work is everything you never wanted. The challenge is that you're constantly doing extra work that you are not being paid extra to do. Since you want to be included, you have mastered the art of faking an enthusiastic smile, being mindful of every word that leaves your mouth, and clapping for ideas that are unimaginative, unhelpful, or, worse, bad for the world.

Most of who you are is hidden. Especially if you don't look like everyone else, you have been careful to fit in in every way possible. So you aren't truly valued or truly seen.

No one is. Everyone is a mere cog in the machine. It is a system of entitlement and resentment.

From the manager's perspective, you get put on a pedestal when you make the company money, make the manager look brilliant, and use the right company lingo—the acronyms, mission statement, and good ole jokes that reveal "I get it, I've been indoctrinated!"

From every employee's perspective, every employee belongs on the pedestal. And from the coworkers looking up from below the pedestal, those on it are to be disliked and pulled down.

People go out of their way to undermine one another. It is dog eat dog, narrowly self-interested, cutthroat. People's personal deformations are being projected onto their relationships with one another.

You think you're not like everyone else, but one day you find yourself critiquing your coworkers on Slack or next to the coffee machine,

making fun of how small-minded they are and laughing with an elitist giggle. Inside, you wince at your own words.
Work is a toxic, exclusive club that you now belong to. *The price of entry was your soul.*

*

You're exhausted, depressed, lost.
You have been running on your own version of a hamster wheel and you can't anymore. You're tired of performing. You feel uninspired and unmotivated.
You can't recall the last time you actually wanted to go to work. Every task feels like the last six miles of a marathon. You have trained for this and know what it takes, but you just don't have the heart to finish.
Suddenly, all of the accolades, awards, and rewards seem like a hot glazed donut after you have already had vanilla cream cake, your favorite ice cream, and decadent chocolate—excessive, overrated, sickening.
You find yourself watching the clock, checking social media, piling and repiling paperwork, and daydreaming about third grade when you didn't know 11:00 a.m. on a Thursday could be this miserable.
You want to keep paying your bills and have something to do every week, but you are fresh out of resilience. *You're burned out.*

*

Your heart aches for a life that you have yet to live but know is still waiting for you.
You followed all the rules. You have done so much for others. The thing is, you submerged yourself in other people's needs and you forgot to form your own identity.
You have no idea who you are.
Life feels like a series of recycled actions with little purpose. Perhaps life has become dull and your hopes and dreams have

5

been shoved into the back of your closet with the jeans you can no longer wear.

You have been doing the same routine for years. You always get up at this time. You always eat this breakfast. You put on this pair of underwear, do that with your hair.

You pick up groceries on this day. You help your kids with their homework. You give them hugs when they need them and you yell, "stop," "no," "yes," "just do it!"

You meet up with your best friends for happy hour and complain about how busy you are and swap skin-care regimens or sports references. You catch season 2 of one of your favorite shows.

You go to the same beach every year and post the obligatory photos: the ocean, drink in hand, the evening you dressed up in the outfit you bought just for this trip.

Suddenly, one day, you're doing something as simple as brushing your teeth, and a wave of overwhelming sadness washes over you.

Your daily schedule is more basic than the Zone bar you had for breakfast.

You have an itch for more. *You realize there's a difference between not being dead and being fully alive.*

*

Your life changed in an instant.

The doctor looked at you and said scary words that made you feel disconnected from everyone in a single moment. Your body has betrayed you.

Or other words have been uttered that immediately transformed the way you saw your life.

"You're a workaholic. It's the only thing you care about."
"I can't be with you anymore."
"You aren't going to be able to have a child biologically."

"The adoption has failed."

"I have cancer."

"You're fired."

"You need to retire graciously or you will be let go."

Perhaps you stumbled onto the information that you somehow knew already but never wanted to confront. Your partner cheated on you. Your boss lied to you. Your best friend stabbed you in the back. Your family member gutted you.

The case could also be that you are the one who failed. You made a massive mistake or multiple mistakes and you have turned your life upside down.

Or perhaps someone you loved in the most profound, beautiful way died. You had no idea that empty space could be so heavy. You've come undone.

Maybe it's been a few years since they died and you want to honor them by living as they would hope for you but you're not sure how.

No matter your crucible moment, you've had a baptism by fire.

*

Whether you are at a crossroads, are feeling conflicted, have gone through a crucible experience or crisis, or some complex combination, you have realized lately that you can no longer ignore the state of things.

Naturally, you find yourself taking an online quiz or several.

Am I depressed? Burned out? How happy am I compared to others? Is my relationship healthy? Am I a good person? On a scale from 1 to 10, how badly does my life suck?

Or you Google for lists: Best places to live. New hobbies. Fall trends. Jobs with the highest satisfaction rates. Methods for managing stress. Top ten reasons to stay married. Characteristics of a toxic relationship. Ways to change things without pissing everyone off.

Maybe you literally ask Google or ChatGPT what to do:

How much do I need to be able to retire?
How do I deal with a toxic family member?
Am I having a midlife crisis?
Should I move?
Should I quit my job?
Should I take this job?
Should I speak up about what is happening?
Should I forgive?
How often should couples have sex?
When is a relationship over?
How do I best care for my kids?
Should I adopt?
Should I go back to school?

You type the words and scan the screen for insight.

Forty-five minutes and seven articles later, you realize you're late, and, while rushing out the door, you are pretty sure you have that disease you can't pronounce that you read about on WebMD and you are wondering whether you should try a new diet, move to an island to work at a tiki bar, or see a therapist.

Hours later when you are finally alone with your thoughts again, you just do what you always do: have ice cream, chips, a few beers, two glasses of wine, or a bourbon, neat, and binge-watch a show or scroll through social media. They are the two hours of your day that allow you to escape your life and not contemplate how lost you feel.

Because in just a few hours, it will be the middle of the night, *but you will be awake.*

The thing you need most is the thing you can't seem to get—sleep. And it is because the faucet was turned off.

Everything is different now. So you need to figure out what to do.

But the choices are overwhelming. And life is so full. There is very little time to even figure out what to do. And you don't know if you need to change, your circumstances need to change, or both.

*

Whether you're guided by a specific religious tradition, consider yourself spiritual but not religious, or avoid God talk altogether, you have likely uttered this inspired and theologically sophisticated prayer: "Help me."

Sometimes it's the screamed version. Something terrible has happened and you literally find yourself calling out for help even if no one is around. Other times, it's a whispered prayer, the kind spoken in your soul when you are getting dressed.

Believe me, I know this prayer well.

"Hi. I need to keep the car a little longer or get another one," I whispered across the counter to the rental car agent. I didn't even realize I was whispering until she asked me to repeat what I said.

We were in the middle of the pandemic. My closest family members lived hours away, and my closest friend was out of town. I had been traveling for two weeks and hadn't received my COVID rapid test results back yet. Since my then husband and I shared a car, I had rented this one to go on a trip to "collect my thoughts" and, in my distressed, blurry state, didn't have a plan beyond the one thing I knew I had to do.

I was living hour by hour.

"If you bring it back tomorrow, it will be just eleven dollars," she said kindly.

With angst, I asked, "If I drop it off in Austin tomorrow instead, how much is it?"

"One hundred forty-two dollars."

With even more anxiety, I asked another question. "What if I bring it back Saturday? My sister said she can meet me here on Saturday."

"One hundred seventy-two dollars."

"I'm not sure," I murmured. I leaned in closer to the counter, not wanting the other customers or her coworker to hear me. I got about six inches from her face. "I think I'm about to get divorced. We share a car and so I just . . ." The sentence trailed off because I didn't know what else to say. I just cried there next to the counter, overwhelmed by the phone call I was about to make.

I was exhausted from not sleeping the night before. I wasn't wearing any makeup and my hair was a mess.

I was a mess.

With eyes full of mercy, she softly said, "Bring it to this address on Saturday. It will be eleven dollars." She was writing the address on a piece of paper and passing it to me across the counter as she spoke.

I needed grace and compassion, and this woman gave it to me.

I left the rental counter and knew I had to make a phone call from the car. I wanted to go to a parking lot that was relatively empty. But more than that, I wanted it to be a place I wouldn't see often. I did not want to constantly look at the place where I made this call.

I drove to a nearby Starbucks, imagining I would want a coffee afterward because I was already exhausted. But I liked this Starbucks, so I looked for other places to park.

"Not Zoe's Kitchen," I thought. "I love to get pickup from there."

"What about that home store?" I wondered.

"No. Too many cars. Too many people could see me crying in my car."

I drove through those parking lots and down the street and saw a church. I pulled into its large parking lot. There were a bunch of cars near one of its buildings. I supposed those were the cars of staff members. The other building for the church had no cars in front of it.

"This will do," I thought. It was empty enough that I could cry in my car with a little privacy. And churches have been sanctuaries to me my whole life.

I scrolled through my phone's contact list and clicked "husband" and made the call. I was less than ten minutes away. But at the time, the distance seemed like a grace.

The truth is that I didn't know what was best.

I hate chaos. I make to-do lists for every day, so I know basically what each day will look like. I like to know how things will unfold. I enjoy planning. But I couldn't plan how this would go. I could only wait and respond as best as I could to whatever happened. It was terrifying.

I called him, and as the phone rang and rang, my heartbeat got faster and faster. I wanted to hang up and drive to California. I wanted someone else to do this for me. I wanted this to be someone else's life.

He didn't answer.

I ended the call and just sat there in the car in silence wondering how long I would be sitting in a parking lot, waiting.

Agony.

A few minutes later, my phone lit up and he was calling me back. I wanted him to call me back so the agony of uncertainty would end. But when I saw his name on my phone, I wanted to throw my phone in a nearby garbage can. Nothing in me wanted to have this conversation.

I answered.

I had written a note on my phone and read it verbatim. I knew I would never, ever get out the words unless I read them like a script. I was just going to get right to the point. Otherwise, I was not sure I would ever get to the point.

"Hi. I am calling you because I have something really difficult to say. This trip has given me the perspective I needed to live toward my decision to file for divorce."

We talked for roughly eight minutes.

The call ended, and I wept in the driver's seat of my white rental car, in the parking lot of a church I had never been to, in a town I had lived in for just over a year, in the middle of a pandemic.

My life changed in an instant.

I had noticed that a man in his late sixties had gone into the building in front of me while I had been on the phone, and he had just come back out. He got into his car and left.

Then it hit me. This is a Catholic church. They are always open. I assumed he went in there to pray. I wondered if I could.

I have attended, spoken at, and worked within multiple kinds of Christian communities, including Catholic communities, but I have never been a member of a Catholic church. Still, my faith has been strengthened and stretched by friends and mentors—living and long dead—who are Catholic.

I walked across the lot and down the sidewalk in front of the building. I approached the large wooden doors and pushed on one with my elbow per pandemic protocol. It opened. I walked in and the sanctuary was dark but filled with lit candles.

I wandered toward the left side, captivated by a statue of Mary in the front left corner.

As I got closer, I realized there was a place to kneel in front of her and she was surrounded by roses—all kinds of different-colored roses. On both sides of the roses, there were tons of candles, most of them lit.

I knelt before Mary and while I was crying, I whispered, "Mary, mother of Jesus, help me. Please help me. Please help him too. You know what it is to be terrified, to be scared of what will happen next."

I cried some more and then I made sure to say, "I know our situations are very different; yours was more important. But I feel like you get what I am saying, that you know what it is to fear and to need help to keep going."

It's funny now, but back then I just couldn't imagine even one more thing going wrong. The last thing I needed was Mary telling God that I think I know what it's like to be a poor unwed teenager who had never had intercourse, having a baby who was going to be the Messiah.

I was silent for a minute or so. Then I asked again.

"Please help me, Mary. Please help us."

I had never knelt before Mary or talked directly to the mother of God before. It surprised me then as much as it may surprise you now.

Some Protestant Christians believe the Catholic practice of honoring or praying to Mary diverts honor and prayer that should flow to Jesus. I grew up with this understanding. But as I have looked into it, it seems to me Catholics do not regard Mary as a person who eclipses her Son. In actuality, their love for Mary only increases their love for

Jesus. The grace and goodness that filled her are the overflowings of the God who made her and gifted her.

As I look back now, she represented for me bravery and comfort and hope that day in the unfamiliar church. In this moment, she was exactly who I needed. I think God wanted me to be in that parking lot. God wanted me to wander into that sanctuary and find solace in her presence.

I wanted to light a candle, but you were supposed to donate three dollars.

I shuffled through my purse and only had a twenty-dollar bill.

I decided not to give the twenty-dollar bill *and* also not to light a candle. Since I did not have three dollars, I felt I could not light one.

I can't break rules very easily.

And even though I'm sheepish to admit it now, I was too anxious to give away twenty dollars. I had lost so much in the parking lot.

*

"Some things break our hearts but fix our vision," as Billie Eidson tenderly explains.

Sometimes your heart breaks and, though it is painful, you gain perspective.

Sometimes you make a decision that breaks your heart and you see differently afterward.

Sometimes both.

If you wanted a guide who figured out what to do from the comfort of a well-worn recliner, I'm afraid you have picked up the wrong book. However, if you are feeling dazed or undone by the questions you need to answer and you would like a companion for your journey that can resonate with feeling consumed by a difficult decision, you have come to the right book.

I come to you in humility, with hard-won insight, the kind that comes from radical surrender and rigorous self-evaluation.

In recent years I got divorced, left a relatively stable job, and dedicated myself to living alcohol-free. If that sentence made you take a deep breath and think, "Shit, that's a lot," you're welcome.

See? I got you.

I don't want the decisions I made to be viewed as exemplars of wisdom and discernment for all people at all times. Rather, in sharing about the process involved in making these decisions, I want you to know that I have made profoundly difficult decisions and I understand what it is to live in their choppy wake. Even when you have zero doubts about a course of action, the consequences can be challenging. How much more so when you forge ahead with some degree of uncertainty! I have learned to make peace with uncertainty and am eager to share how you can, too.

You can think of me as a kind of sherpa. Sherpas climb mountains with other mountaineers. They know the possible routes since they have climbed the mountains before. But every day on the mountain is different, and everyone has to make their own climb.

Try to see yourself as a discoverer.

The quest to make this decision is not simply about this one thing and what you should do; it's about the larger story of your life. And as you will read later on, this journey involves other people too, and possibly in ways you may not have reflected on yet. In other words, you may feel lonely as you tread the turbulent waters of your life, but you are connected to others and your life is held in a web of mutuality. More on this later.

Some travel tips as we set out on the journey:

You can take the journey alone. But it can be helpful to go on this journey with others—with people with a similar decision or people who are also trying to figure out what to do in their own lives.

Give yourself time. If this is a life-altering decision, be patient with yourself. Let yourself be unsure for a while. Perhaps read these words aloud to yourself, "I will go on the journey this book invites and give myself permission to slowly but surely figure out what to do. I will engage with this book's invitations and truly allow God to speak to me."

Trust the process. You can get unstuck and grow. Each chapter of this book will give you a next thing to do, ways of listening for God, examining emerging possibilities and pathways, and choosing a wise way forward.

At any point in the journey toward figuring out what to do, actually doing it, and living with your new story, you can say this prayer: Help me. It reminds you that help outside of yourself is there. Think of this prayer as a kind of anchor for your soul, a gentle reminder that you are seen, heard, and held.

As you take some time to figure out what to do next, be gentle with yourself and try to even enjoy the process of discovery.

*

Fear tries to convince you to protect yourself from anything that could possibly go awry while on this journey. Fear whispers that you will surely do the wrong thing, mess up your life, and never find the life you were meant to live.

You don't need to fear asking questions.

You are in the liminal space between not knowing what to do and knowing what to do. Asking a hard, big question is not the same thing as making a significant decision.

At this stage of your journey, you are simply acknowledging openly that you feel a stirring, you feel unsure, and you need help figuring out what to do.

If you are feeling unsettled, unfulfilled, or undone, you owe it to yourself, to the life God imagines for you, to the Spirit of God, who prompts and guides you, to constructively work through what is churning within you.

Scholar Elaine James notes that the Bible's wisdom books suggest that when we feel an irrepressible energy within, it is an energy that is simultaneously divine and human.

Well-known and lesser-known saints have felt such a willful stirring. Throughout this book, I will tell the stories of multiple people who have experienced a stirring they could not ignore, made difficult changes, and lived into a new story. Allow their stories to inspire you.

Civil rights activist and theologian Howard Thurman encourages,

Look well to the growing edge! All around us worlds are dying and new worlds are being born; all around us life is dying and life is being born. The fruit ripens on the tree, the roots are silently at work in the darkness of the earth against a time when there shall be new leaves, fresh blossoms, green fruit. Such is the growing edge! It is the extra breath from the exhausted lung, the one more thing to try when all else has failed, the upward reach of life when weariness closes in upon all endeavor. This is the basis of hope in moments of despair, the incentive to carry on when times are out of joint and [humans] have lost their reason, the source of confidence when worlds crash and dreams whiten into ash. The birth of a child—life's most dramatic answer to death—this is the growing edge incarnate. Look well to the growing edge!

You can give yourself permission to grow.

You can change your mind.

You don't have to be the same person you were ten years ago or even a year ago. You don't have to be the constant in your family, your friend group, your workplace, your anything.

On the other hand, a life-altering change to your circumstances is not necessary for you to grow. The point of this journey is not to ensure you change your life in a significant way—not all change is progress. The point is for you to move toward God's presence, toward wholeness, healing, love.

Maybe your soul simply needs to reconnect with its aliveness. Perhaps this is a journey for taking up a different value or discarding something you've believed to be true that is no longer helpful. Maybe this journey will encourage a subtle shift in your perspective or engagement with a new habit.

If the words of this book are resonating with you, there is a stirring within you that must be attended to.

I believe in you. You are brave enough and strong enough to figure this out.

FIELD NOTES TO SELF

- Adopt the posture of an explorer. Embrace curiosity.
- Consider finding a partner or group to journey alongside.
- Give yourself permission to change.

SURRENDERING

When You Feel Worried, Stuck, Powerless

Transitions can only take place if we are willing to let go of what we have known, the worlds we have created, and our assumptions about "how things are." To let go is the precursor to being reborn.

—Barbara A. Holmes, *Crisis Contemplation*

Iñigo de Loyola was born in 1491 in northern Spain. Iñigo was a brilliant soldier with a bright future in the military. At one point, he and others believed he would one day be a general.

But all of that changed in a tragic moment.

Before the age of thirty, he was hit by a cannonball that shattered the bone of his right leg and lacerated his left calf.

Iñigo went through grueling surgery, and afterward his right leg was shorter than the left. Then he went through another painful surgery trying to correct it, which only made it worse. He was bedridden for many months. Along with his physical health, he lost his career, the vision he had for his future, and his sense of meaning and purpose.

The only thing Iñigo had felt deeply enthusiastic about was taken from him.

But over time, through his fragility and openness, a new vision for his life, a choice he had not seen before, emerged.

He wanted something to do during his challenging recovery, so he asked for books about his favorite subject, chivalry. Even while lying there, he was having trouble letting go of his dream since chivalry is a system of behaviors and qualities of knights that was outside the capacities of his injured body.

Yet the only books available were ones about the life of Jesus and stories about saints like Francis of Assisi, a man who gave up his wealth and family connections to become an itinerant preacher and live with and love the poor.

To his great surprise, Iñigo became inspired by the saints' lives and suddenly felt like God was guiding him toward something new.

In order to figure out what to do next, he took a pilgrimage, and one of the places he went was Montserrat. Montserrat is a multi-peaked mountain above the city of Barcelona in Spain. Pilgrims have traveled to the monastery on the mountain for hundreds of years. Nestled amid the magnificent peaks is a chapel that displays Our Lady of Montserrat, a black and gold statue of the Virgin Mary. It's one of the most famous black Madonnas in the world.

Iñigo spent the night kneeling in prayer. There, he surrendered his sword, sword belt, and dagger and left it all in front of her.

Iñigo later described being given a vision of victory in life with new kinds of weapons—prayer and humility. After he surrendered his sword, he continued on his pilgrimage, where he experienced depression and spiritual trials coupled with meaningful encounters with God.

His personal journey inspired him to create spiritual exercises that have shaped people's spirituality and helped people make decisions for over five hundred years—including me.

I didn't know about his pilgrimage to Montserrat and what happened there until after I began learning more about his life and how he made decisions. When I realized he had also knelt before an image of Mary and prayed in the midst of intense change in his life, I felt even more connected with his story.

Mysteriously, his journey began to animate mine.

Ignatius of Loyola, as he is now known, went on to found the Society of Jesus. And the Jesuits continue his mission around the world to this day.

As I have studied the lives of people like Ignatius who have made difficult decisions and transitions in their lives, I have noticed how all of them had a stage of complete fragility. For Ignatius, this fragility was literal. He had to lie in a bed while his body healed and reimagine his life.

If we are to settle the stirring within, each of us, in our own way, needs to surrender.

Here's what you will discover: your fragility is a form of power.

Question: Where do I start?
Prayer: Be with me.

I pressed my fingertips and heels more deeply into the floor. Listening closely for the next direction, I tried to take a deep breath.

But I couldn't.

It was so hard to breathe. It's all I wanted, just to breathe in and out freely and feel okay.

It was the summer of 2020, the summer when we tried to do everything we were used to doing in ways we had never dreamed of doing them. Due to the global pandemic, we were all overwhelmed.

I was in my homemade gym. I have loved lifting weights and doing different types of workouts for years as a form of stress relief. Losing access to a gym was like losing access to medication for mental distress. My gym had been a lifeline.

So, like many other people, I went online and bought some weights and a bench and a few other pieces of gear and did my best to move my body in this room once a day to find a sense of peace.

I had also started following online yoga videos, specifically *Yoga with Adriene*, and with deep gratitude discovered a form of moving my body that helped my heart and mind too. But on this day, the peace I sought could not be felt on this mat.

The more I tried to power through the video, *the more powerless I felt.*

It wasn't just the pandemic that weighed on me. It was nearly every aspect of my life. It was how I felt as though my soul had a cavity. It was the drinking I was doing to cope with it all, something that dulled the ache for a time but ultimately caused further internal turmoil.

I had tried so many things—therapy, prayers, journaling, reading special books and articles, taking on new habits, listening to podcasts, trying to get more sleep, building this home gym—and still I found myself on this mat, trying to catch my breath, and feeling completely vulnerable.

I suddenly lay on my face and whispered, "I surrender."

*

I've spent most of my life trying to rely on others in the loosest possible way. I loved to help others. I hated to ask for help.

I have also always hated the phrase "Let go and let God," until recently too. It seemed ridiculous. My thinking has always gone something like this: If I don't keep holding on to this, everything will fall apart. I am the manager of all things. I am the timekeeper, the careful eye, the person who makes sure stuff gets done.

I used to think letting go meant a free-for-all, welcoming a mess that I would eventually have to clean up. I believed that without me controlling everything, the universe, my universe specifically, would not run.

I've often whispered some version of "God, you seem trustworthy and powerful and all, but you have a lot to think about, many prayers to respond to, and if I am honest, sometimes the way you handle stuff is not the way I would do it."

Therefore, most of my life, I semi-let God and never let go. I *almost* gave it over. I asked God for co-help.

If I'm honest, I usually offered God the parts I already had covered.

But that day on the mat I dropped it all. What I was carrying was so heavy that I had to let go. I could not hold it all anymore.

I am still living in this pose today—dependent, vulnerable, humble.

That day on a blue mat in my homemade gym I exhaled. I stopped clinching my hands and holding my breath. My body went limp. I acknowledged how I felt and let myself feel those feelings deeply. I stopped the mental gymnastics. No more sweeping things under the rug. I had to tell God and other people I needed help. I could no longer keep up the charade of self-reliance and know-how.

I didn't know how.

That was the first truth I had to acknowledge. And that initial act of surrender opened a new option: living truthfully rather than keeping up appearances of having it all together.

My drive to please people at all costs sputtered. I became more interested in cultivating actual peace than in keeping the peace. And I cared more about making things right than pretending things were all right.

This meant living honestly with myself, others, and God. Out loud.

I'm lonely.
I'm afraid.
I'm unsure.
I'm confused.
I'm hurt.
There is a problem.
I won't do this anymore.
No.
I feel pulled in multiple directions.
Things aren't going well.
I'm not well.

My holistic surrender and desire to live honestly and work on things in my life led to insights.

I have many parts within me. Each is important and trying to support or protect me. I can listen to the various parts of me, even if it seems they are at odds with one another, and hear what they yearn for.

Following my own surrender, I learned a lot.

I could acknowledge problems without assuming they would usher in chaos, an enduring fear of mine. But if chaos ensued, I could deal with it appropriately.

Having hard conversations is part of life. Hard conversations are not tragedies.

It is possible to acknowledge wrongdoing on my part without feeling shame or self-hatred.

I have limitations; some I can work on and some I need to learn to live with.

The day on the yoga mat was six months before I knelt in front of Mary, praying for help. So life did not simply get easier after surrender.

Yet as I have come to know this way of moving through the world, I have dealt with uncertainty and difficult emotions head-on *and* I have felt freer, slept deeper, stood up for myself more, owned my weaknesses, lived into my strengths, had better boundaries, and sought God more.

I feel more alive than I have in a long time.

I am more fully human this way.

*

Of all of the interviews I did for this book, I deeply connected to Lydia's story. From the moment Lydia was given the job, it didn't feel quite right.

But she was supposed to be living the dream. She moved her family to San Diego for this job, one of the most beautiful cities in the United States, with its sunny, warm weather and epic coastline.

This was a substantial promotion, especially at her age. Her job was to lead a prominent, large congregation with multiple staff members, which is comparable to being the CEO of a sought-after company.

As if this was not enough, Lydia was the first Asian American female given the role and the youngest person to ever be appointed. She felt like she should consider herself lucky. A lot of people expected great things from her and were excited about the new direction she would take this church in.

Yet the nagging feeling that she wasn't in the right place was ever present.

Lydia tried multiple methods to change her perspective on what was happening within her. She kept thinking it was a flaw in her that she wasn't fully present to her new role.

And she had powerful questions that created a stressful struggle within:

Am I going to ruin my reputation?

What will happen next?

What am I escaping?

What will happen to our finances?

If I leave, will I miss out on a really good opportunity for me?

Am I not giving myself enough time to adjust to this new appointment and city?

Am I the kind of person who is dissatisfied anywhere I go?

On top of these perplexing questions to answer, people's expectations weighed on her. She likes to make other people happy. And if she left, especially so soon after arriving, people would be disappointed, maybe worse.

But one day she realized she couldn't force herself to want to be in San Diego, in this position.

She needed to admit how she felt to herself and to the people she loves.

What began as a feeling of initial resistance turned into regular prayer, journaling, and conversations with her clergy coach, husband, and other family members about wanting to leave the position.

And as she admitted what she was feeling, something strange happened.

As she honestly and openly declared how she felt with God, herself, and people she trusts, she realized she was giving herself freedom to figure out what to do.

What was incredible is that Lydia realized that honestly declaring what was stirring within her did not automatically mean she was going to change something. It wasn't inevitable that she would leave her job or move from San Diego. It simply meant that she was now free to actually make a decision, to become wildly introspective, to invite feedback from people on what she was feeling, to get guidance from God.

*

One way of going through life is to bear our way through it and frantically cling to our ways of knowing, being, acting, and wanting. *The other way of going through life is to move with it and continuously surrender.*

Surrender is an "inner attitude" that accepts what is and accepts our current inability to see the future.

Acceptance doesn't mean we like or consent to our circumstances as they are. Far from it! But rather than fight, flee, numb ourselves, or fearfully maintain the status quo, we choose to sit with our life as it is.

We can repeat phrases to ourselves such as:

"At this moment, my life is like this."
"I wish this had different timing, but this is what it is."
"I do not like this, but it is what it is right now."
"I am afraid. I don't want things to change and I can't live like this much longer."

I find it helpful to actually write down phrases related to surrender and post them behind cabinet doors and in drawers throughout my house; they are little reminders to keep letting go. I choose to use colorful, sticky notepaper.

Some of mine are:

Detach to attach well
Don't avoid, accept

Go ahead and grab some paper and write down two phrases right now that will encourage you daily or make a note to yourself to do it soon.

Instead of waking each day aiming to fix, manage, firefight, control, or change your situation, or spend the day being anxious about it, avoiding it, or convincing yourself to find the good in it, like it, or grit through it, I invite you to decide right now to enter a new way of existing in your daily life by practicing surrender.

Accept that you are exhausted and have no more moves left.

Or if what I have written does not resonate, whatever it is that you're feeling, thinking, experiencing, *accept* those feelings, thoughts, and experiences.

Beyond engaging in honesty and acceptance, practicing surrender means recognizing you have come to the end of your knowledge and skills. The good news is that "I don't know" creates space for imagining and learning.

Cameron Trimble explains it this way, "By getting lost and welcoming the reality that we do not have the answers or know the way forward, we enter a space of liminality and emergence. We are not attempting to fix 'broken systems' but are, instead, summoning entirely new worlds."

Surrender is also an act of trust, of faith.

"Faith, on the other hand, is an unreserved opening of the mind to the truth, whatever it may turn out to be. Faith has no preconceptions; it is a plunge into the unknown. Belief clings, but faith lets go," writes Alan Watts.

Surrender literally means to give back, return, restore.

The word "render" is in the word "surrender." When we render things, we submit them for judgment or inspection. Likewise, rendering is a process of melting down for the sake of clarifying and purifying.

Offer up what is happening to God; submit it for examination.

Interior surrender isn't about passivity. Instead, like Cynthia Bourgeault writes, "interior surrender is often precisely what makes it possible to see a decisive action that must be taken and to do it with courage and strength."

As we detach from particular outcomes, negative what-ifs, and predictions, we open ourselves to new possibilities, positive what-ifs, and prudence. *As we surrender, we open ourselves to wisdom.*

*

White and brown columns of the colossal cathedral surround the area where the service is happening. The ceilings are sixty-nine feet high and painted blue with a yellow and white bursting sunshine in the middle. Every inch of the walls is covered in color and magnificent imagery. Even the space preaches.

My dear friend Liz is in a simple, oversized white robe, lying with her face on the floor. Several other people are lying alongside her. Together, they form a circle, all of them facing inward on their stomachs. They cover one hand with the other and place their foreheads onto the back of their stacked hands. They are "candidates for holy orders" in the Christian Episcopal denomination, and this is their ordination service.

This is the day when they commit their work and their lives in service to God and the church. It's a kind of wedding ceremony. As Liz lies on her face in front of all of us, I think of how vulnerable she looks. She can't see what is behind her or in front of her. She can barely lift her head. She cannot even crawl from this position. There is no movement forward or backward, just stillness and a yielding to all that is and is to come.

This is one mode of absolute surrender.

She is giving herself over to something larger than herself, the community around her, the leadership of those who have more wisdom and experience than her, the saints of her tradition, living and dead, who have shown her the way, the God who created all things, and she is giving herself to the Great Story being told—that story that each of us is held within, contributes to, and can draw strength from.

*

Practicing surrender in a physical way will help to open yourself to this journey. There are many forms of bodily surrender.

You can physically prostrate yourself like Liz. You can literally lie on your stomach and fold your hands over one another and put your forehead on them. I did a version of this pose when I surrendered. I collapsed onto my yoga mat face-first, and tears covered the back of my hands.

You could also lie on your back with your hands at your sides or with one hand on your belly and one hand on your heart. Allow your legs to be comfortably outstretched.

You can also sit on your knees, with your heels under your bum. I recommend having thick carpet or a rolled-up blanket under your knees if you're over thirty-five.

I always feel like a kid when I sit like this. And that is the point. This position opens me to childlike wonder, reminds me that the world is something to be in awe of, and helps me to engage my curiosity and imagination.

As you sit on your knees or in a chair or your wheelchair, you can put your hands out in front of you, palms up. In one hand, imagine putting everything that you are currently facing and visualize it sitting there. In your other hand, put your difficult feelings, expectations, what-ifs, predictions. Picture it all sitting there. And then flip your hands over.

Offer it all.

If you let it, these forms of physical surrender can allow you to find a bit of rest in between not knowing what to do and doing something.

It can allow you to relax into your unknowing.

In the midst of this difficult decision, you can make it a habit to regularly lie on your stomach or your back or sit, hands out, and imagine yourself finding respite and consolation in the arms of God.

Feel the ground, bed, or seat beneath you and realize, "I am being held. I don't have to go anywhere right now. I am okay in this moment."

It may feel like you are doing nothing.

It's like prayer. People often think prayer is what happens before or after something, but the prayer is also *a something*. It's an action that draws attention, moves us, connects, can be felt by others, centers, calms, nurtures, teaches, guides. It is doing something meaningful even when we aren't entirely aware of what is happening.

The same is true of surrender.

*

Once Lydia admitted what she was thinking and feeling and accepted what she was experiencing, she sought guidance in various forms.

One of the things she did was to listen to podcast episodes on making hard decisions and charting new paths. A particular episode that meant a lot to her asked, "If every option has the best result, which would you choose?" She was incredibly encouraged by this question. She had mostly been considering everything that could go wrong instead.

In addition to being a pastor, Lydia is also a writer, so she had more than one job at the time and was regularly writing articles, meditations, and workbooks.

One day while praying about her situation, she found herself saying to God, "If it is okay that I leave, give me a sign."

Out of the blue, a well-known author, creator, and speaker reached out to her about being on his podcast. She took this as a sign that her writing could sustain her, even if for a little while. And that God was saying to her that it was okay to resign. She decided to trust her own instincts and to believe in herself.

Just ten months into the new job, she made the decision to leave. As she had imagined, people were disappointed. But it didn't ruin her reputation.

She lives in a new city that she has always felt mystically connected to, and, to her own surprise, she eventually accepted a new role in a different church.

Lydia sees leaving the job in San Diego as the best decision she has ever made.

FIELD NOTES TO SELF

- Practice surrender.
- Lean into the unknown.
- Cultivate space for imagining and learning.

SEEKING

When You Don't Know Who to Trust and Listen To

"God
Whatever you want to say
I'm here
I'm listening."

—Amena Brown, in *A Rhythm of Prayer*

We circled up on the cream rug with tan and brown swirls in my living room, standing close to one another. We could hear each other breathing—several of us, deeply. It was spring of 2022, and, given the COVID-19 pandemic, it had been two years since any of us had stood this close to other people, holding hands.

I chose someone to open with prayer and said I would close out the prayer time. I encouraged anyone who felt led to pray in between. Intimate "popcorn" prayers burst out from a place we hadn't accessed in a while. They were the kinds of prayers that we don't usually say in front of other people.

After the time of prayer, I could feel my palms were moist with human contact. Usually, it would kind of gross me out. This time, it was the most comforting thing I had felt in months. The greatest gift the pandemic gave me was a newfound appreciation for deep presence with other people.

Everyone in this group had one thing in common: they were trying to figure out what to do. Each of us had a stirring, something that was keeping us awake at night that brought us together.

So we decided to meet in my living room every couple of weeks for the rest of the semester. At the time, I was still a professor, and so time ticked by in semesters. The plan was simple. I would open with a poem, a quote, or a story from the Bible, and then I would pose a question. Then anyone could talk for as long as they liked about the question or whatever else came to their lips.

This was the first night of the first week this group met up. And we talked about Bartimaeus.

One of my favorite stories about Jesus is when he meets a man named Bartimaeus who is blind by the roadside. As Jesus passes by, he asks Jesus to have mercy on him. Jesus turns toward him and asks, "What do you want me to do for you?"

Bartimaeus replies, "I want to see."

I turned to everyone in the group and asked the same question Jesus had asked.

"What do you want God to do for you?"

Each person had come with lived experience that was heavy to carry—health struggles, spiritual abuse, sexual harassment, identity questions, blurry futures—yet it took several minutes for the first person to find an answer to this question.

For many of us, what we wanted God to do was somewhat different from the story we came to tell. As we sifted through the differences, slight as they may have been, "lady wisdom" showed up.

In the book of Proverbs, wisdom is depicted as a woman who has invited you to dine at her table at her extravagant house.

> Lady Wisdom goes to town, stands in a
> prominent place,
> and invites everyone within sound of her voice:
> "Are you confused about life, don't know what's
> going on?
> Come with me, oh come, have dinner with me!
> I've prepared a wonderful spread—fresh-baked bread,
> roast lamb, carefully selected wines.
> Leave your impoverished confusion and *live*!
> Walk up the street to a life with meaning."

Over the weeks, through our collective grief, desire for connection, honest discussions, and prayers, God became more obvious, more real, more able. And as we witnessed one another's wrestling, things mystically became clearer. Not to say that each person walked away with a decision made, but there was a kind of healing that took place in walking with one another so that even if things still felt somewhat open, we were more comfortable with being uncomfortable.

And we felt less alone. Never underestimate the power of feeling less alone. That in itself will help you tremendously on this journey.

I know of communities who do similar forms of group spiritual direction and discernment. Some spend a good amount of time in prayer and silence and then share images or words for the person they are helping at the end of the time.

The Quaker religious tradition has "clearness committees" to help individuals discover whether there is clarity to move forward with a matter, wait, or take another action. The group worships together, and then they listen deeply to the questions and concerns brought by the individual they are helping. Finally, they spend a few hours asking the person open, honest questions in a gentle way.

God shows up in questions, dialogue, and times of silence.

It will be incredibly helpful to find a community of people (whether everyone is helping you or everyone is helping everyone) where there is space for deep listening and support, even if just for a few hours. If you want to form your own group, you will find an exercise in the appendix with guidance for what to do together.

> *Question: Who should I ask for advice?*
> *Prayer: Speak to me.*

Frederick Douglass is best known for escaping slavery and becoming a national leader of the abolitionist movement, but what it took to make the decisions to flee and fight for his liberation and the freedom of others is less well-known.

Douglass had been indoctrinated to believe he was serving God through slavery, his duty. Over time, he learned to read and was introduced to new views. Specifically, *The Columbian Orator*, a collection of essays, dialogues, and poetry, denounced slavery and oppression and began to change his perspective on his life experiences. Before this, he didn't have words for his curiosity, concerns, or sadness about his life.

In his autobiography, Douglass writes, "The reading of these speeches added much to my limited stock of knowledge, and enabled me to give tongue to many interesting thoughts which had often flashed through my mind and died away for want of words in which to give them utterance."

Over time, it became clear through study and prayer that slavery wasn't God's intention for any human being.

Douglass began meeting with trusted friends to figure out whether and how to escape bondage and seize the freedom they all knew they deserved.

"Pending the time of our contemplated departure out of Egypt, we met often by night, and on every Sunday," he wrote. "At these meetings we talked the matter over, told our hopes and fears, and the difficulties discovered or imagined; and like men of sense, counted the cost of the enterprise to which we were committing ourselves."

Douglass's group had to wrestle with their emotions during their process, too. "We were, at times, confident, bold, and determined, and again, doubting, timid, and wavering." Though markedly different, and likely with much more severe possible consequences than most decisions, Douglass's group offers helpful advice for any individual or group who is making a difficult decision.

- Explore your thoughts about what you are experiencing. Talk it out with others. Name anything and everything that is coming up for you.
- Share your hopes and your fears. What are the best possible outcomes? What are your greatest aspirations? Which are imagined fears and which are realistic?
- With others, name what difficulties are present now and what could become difficult later and consider together how to navigate these difficulties.
- Count the cost. Is what you might gain more important than what you might lose?

*

When you are seeking guidance and advice, it can be hard to know who to trust and whom to listen to. The best companions during this journey are people whom you can trust enough to be your authentic self around, so you can share your confusion, hopes, fears, and questions without judgment.

It's also helpful to connect with others who know what matters to you and care about your holistic well-being. They know something of your values and what moves you and makes you who you are. You are looking for people who will encourage you and give you strength.

Find people who know how to "hold space." These are people who know how to sit with you in the uncomfortable in-between space of not knowing what to do and doing something. People like this are not quick to assume how you should respond. They don't dismiss your feelings or your bodily reactions (your tears, sighs, or anything else). Great companions are like those in a Quaker clearness committee, people who don't simply give advice but help you to ask better, deeper questions.

It's wise to talk with people who are lifelong learners and move through life with humility. These are people who have convictions, but they are willing to be wrong and to change.

It is good to have a balance of people with *high stakes* in your decision (because likely they know you well and really care about the outcome) and people who have *little to no stakes* in your decision, who will be even more open-minded and curious.

When I was trying to decide whether to leave my academic job, a colleague and friend, Justin, asked me a set of incredible questions. Justin and I had only hung out a few times, but he knew the nature of my decision well, what I was choosing between. He had no stakes in my staying or going, but he cared about my well-being and he wanted to create space to help me think through my decision on a particular afternoon.

At this point, I was pretty sure I would resign, but several options were on the table.

> What would you be giving up that is helpful to you? And how will you solve for it?
> What kind of community would sustain you?
> How will you stay stimulated and challenged?
> Is there any sense in which you will still be trying to prove yourself? If so, is that a problem?
> Are you trying to prove yourself in such a way that God will use it for your good and the good of the world?

His questions were wildly helpful because they mitigated fears I had and helped me to realize I could picture possible paths as well as potential problems and, with God's help, creativity, and thought, could make smaller decisions that would help me with my larger, looming decision. I felt at peace while we talked and while I jotted down his questions. I felt heard and I felt challenged in an incredibly helpful way.

While we don't want to feel judged or shamed during our processing, we also want to be careful not to create an echo chamber around ourselves so that we are only being fed what we want to hear and what we already care about or agree with or want.

It is easy for us to see what our community sees and very hard to see something our community doesn't see or doesn't want to see. Also, if I like someone and if I feel comfortable around them, and they tell me something, it's much easier for me to believe it. We tend to reward people we like with belief. We are prone to disbelieve the truth that comes from an unfamiliar person or a person we don't feel comfortable around.

Are there people you need to nurture connection with who can help you to see what is happening in ways you haven't considered yet or to see something you need to see and is hidden?

Sometimes people will have conflicting thoughts for us, or what they will say will conflict with what we have been thinking. Disagreement or contending ideas are helpful for our journey too. As for people with different paths than us, their experiences can inform our own grappling. It can feed our imaginations about both what is possible and what isn't good for us.

*

"Secrets make you sick," Marcus said. As I interviewed Marcus about some of the most painful moments of his life, I knew instantly that his vulnerability and courage would help others.

Shortly after getting married and being accepted into a PhD program, Marcus suddenly realized he was struggling with severe depression. He isolated himself. He couldn't write, even with looming deadlines.

He had always loved being with people and writing, and he was living his dreams, so none of this made any sense.

He told me he remembered thinking, "This is everything I ever wanted. I have a wonderful church. I just got married. I am in the program I wanted to be in. I don't have to relocate."

Yet he was also questioning whether he wanted to live or not.

Once he started the PhD program, he felt like he was going into class as half of a person. He said, "It looked like I didn't care about school, but in reality, I didn't want to be alive. I felt like I was wasting away."

Marcus didn't know whether to talk with his wife or not because she is a mental health professional and he didn't want to add to her stress. He knows about the daily trauma she encounters and sees her come home regularly feeling defeated.

"I can't tell her any of this because it will just compound things," he had thought. His cultural background and family history only made it harder for him to discern whether to reach out for help.

He told me, "Hispanic families don't deal well with these things." And he has always seen himself as self-sufficient. "Standing on my own two feet is how I move through life," he said. For Marcus, this came through watching his parents. His dad was in the military and deployed a lot. His mom was obligated to just press forward because there was no other option. "She needed to be the person that handled everything." Marcus felt similarly during this time.

He knew he wasn't all right, but questions swirled in his head. Was he going to let his spouse down? Was he going to let his professors down?

The most difficult thing was the extreme highs and lows. Some days he could envision himself doing grand projects and would stay up for nights seizing the moment. Other days, he crashed. He told me during the worst times, he would lock himself in the bathroom. "I felt like I was on a bridge, ten thousand feet up, looking down. That's the sinking feeling I had."

Eventually, he opened up to his wife, who thought he might have bipolar. With her encouragement, he sought mental health care. All the diagnoses came back positive for bipolar 2. He started taking a low dose of antidepressants and kept thinking things would get better. But he was still having bouts of hypomania and depression.

At one point when he was desperately trying to write a paper, he wondered if he should reach out again. "I was at a friend's house and confided in them and asked what I should do. I asked, 'Should I text my advisor even though it's the middle of the night?' My friend encouraged me that my advisor needed to know what was going on."

Marcus listened to his friend and texted his trusted advisor. "I almost did something that would have done irreversible damage. I need help. I want to get better."

His advisor called him and asked him a powerful question, "Do you need time?" This wasn't something he had considered yet. With the encouragement and help of his advisor, he was able to make the difficult decision to take time away from graduate school to focus on his mental health.

It took a care network of people to help make the decision to take a break. "I needed my wife to tell me to get a diagnosis. I needed a friend to tell me to send the text. I needed my advisor to ask me a powerful question and encourage me to get help," he explained. After reflecting on the insight he has gained, he said, "I got picked up by a lot of people. It is not a burden to reach out to people and say I'm lonely, I'm afraid."

*

No matter who you talk with, you will want to be careful to attend your feelings, heart, body, and God's voice and direction as you listen to them.

Some people come out of the woodwork during a crisis. There are the "fixers" who need to know for themselves that they did something to try and help. Even if unhelpful and unsuccessful, they can sleep at night because "at least they tried."

Others have their own agendas. They can't imagine their life changing because of a decision you might make. So, they try to make sure you don't do something that will create emotional, mental, or relational work for them.

Other people have gone through something similar and will project their experience and feelings onto you and want you to make the same decision that they did:

Get the divorce.
Stay married.
Retire.
Don't retire.
Quit your job! Who needs them?!
Don't start your own business!
Get that treatment!
Don't believe them!
And on and on . . .

As people try to help you, listen for the inner voice that says: This person has my best interest at heart and is asking important questions and deeply listening. This person is genuinely open and will do their best to help me to hear God's guidance and do the next right thing.

*

Marcus is still navigating mental health challenges, and it is his community that sustains his life.

"I come back to the people who love me. That's what grounds me. In group therapy, I feel the Spirit's presence and see them as saints. I see the people at church every Sunday as saints too. That is where my religious ideals are embodied. Religion becomes real for me when it is experienced with other people."

Thankfully, the clouds have parted enough for Marcus to realize, "God isn't finished with me yet."

Eventually, after taking a break and returning, Marcus had to decide whether to leave the PhD program altogether or fight to get back into it after the system neglected to help him in the ways he needed.

Marcus turned in a final paper late, after enduring a hypomanic episode, and was told by a professor that he had earned a failing grade. In this case, when Marcus needed to be writing, he was spending multiple hours searching for rocks. He had a vision that he needed to be finding the right rocks. He promptly bought a headlamp and was searching frantically all day for the right ones.

Marcus tried to explain what happened, but the professor didn't fully understand what it's like for Marcus to live with bipolar 2.

Marcus and his advisor went on to meet with the office of student learning to try and explore every available option. He eventually realized that even this office had no structure in place to truly support graduate students who have mental health issues.

Marcus knew he had an option to appeal, but his advisor warned it would be a bureaucratic mess and an uphill battle. And with all that he was already navigating, it felt like too much. As he thinks back, he feels like these were possibly signs that he needed to let go. Ultimately, Marcus decided to leave the program and focus on learning to live well with bipolar 2.

Sometimes difficult decisions are made in relationship to a muddled and hurtful combination of people who deeply understand and people who absolutely don't.

Marcus was sad to let go of this lifelong dream and also felt like it was the right thing to do.

*

This journey needs you *and* companions.

You can trust yourself *and* others to help you to figure this out.

Nearly everyone who has forged a new path for themselves had mentors or models. They were compelled by the lives of others. As I did for this book, you can read the biographies and autobiographies of brave people who have made bold choices. There is a list of resources on my website (www.angelagorrell.com).

As you engage the stories of people past and present, listen for their questions, their process, and the ways they came to know what to do. Let them inspire you and give you fresh perspective. How did they figure out what to do? What happened? And allow yourself to imagine similar possibilities on your own decision journey.

Sometimes you will figure out what to do when you least expect it.

*

During our phone interview, Carol sounded like a woman who was content. I was eager to hear why. Carol had been working more than fifty years, part time since she was fifteen, and full time since she was just eighteen. "It was my existence," she told me.

For two years, she wondered whether she should retire, and the decision was difficult because it wasn't obvious what would bring her peace. She was prepared financially but still found it hard to give up an annual salary.

The unknowns made it especially difficult. Her workplace was where she shined and was fed, so she wondered how she would feel not having that anymore. Other questions deepened her confusion. What will I do with my time? Will I be productive? "The decision built and built in my mind," she recalled.

For months, Carol meditated and prayed about what to do. She had talks with herself and others. She told me that the least helpful type of conversation she had was with people who had retired! Some people loved it, others hated it, which only confused her more.

One Sunday morning she was at church. She has been a part of the worship band at her church for years, and band members were hanging out together between rehearsal and the service. Out of the blue, the drummer in the band asked, "Carol, why are you still working?"

She said, "I like my job. It's close to where I live. I still feel good."

He responded, "Do you want to work until you don't feel good?"

And suddenly she thought, "No. I don't."

It was like a lightbulb went off. Images of how she wanted to spend her time beyond working flashed in her mind. "I want to hike. I want to travel," she remembered thinking.

For Carol, this question, not advice or an answer, was heaven-sent, divine.

"It was in church. I don't think it was a coincidence, where I was, who I was talking to, the lightness I felt afterward," she explained. Given that she had been praying and meditating for months on what to do, she felt like this was God's release from work for her. It immediately took the heaviness off her shoulders.

Before she talked to her boss about her plan to retire, she did her homework. She met with her financial advisor. She imagined potential roadblocks to her feeling content about this decision and preemptively took care of them. She made concrete plans for travel with friends and increased her involvement in church. And she also took up walking, preparing to hike more often.

In the last year, Carol has traveled to Nashville and Santa Fe to see friends. She also took a road trip with two of her best friends to Louisiana. She now gets to visit her sister weekly. During our conversation she said, "Tomorrow, I am going to the LA County Museum of Art in the middle of the week! I am discovering new places in my neighborhood just by walking it. I've been grateful ever since [I retired] and never regretted it. It's been amazing."

As God did for Carol, who was faithfully seeking God's guidance for a time, God places people in our lives that are "living signs" that point us to him.

FIELD NOTES TO SELF

- Ask God to speak to you through others.
- Seek out people who will ask you compelling questions.
- Other people's stories can encourage and help you name new possibilities.

SENSING

When You Feel Difficult Feelings

Untamed fear consumes you, becomes you, until what you are most afraid of turns alive.

—Suleika Jaouad, *Between Two Kingdoms*

It may surprise you to find out that Fred Rogers, beloved for his pioneering television show *Mister Rogers' Neighborhood*, grew up in a very wealthy family. They were the type of rich family who had a cook and other household staff. They went on luxurious vacations and had more than one beautiful home.

Fred's parents were also very committed to their Presbyterian church and to philanthropy, both of which also had a huge influence on his life and work. Fred's childhood friend, Anita Manolo, credits his parents' modesty and humility with developing his character. His mom took care of the needs of so many families in their community that eventually the school nurse of their local elementary school would just buy whatever kids needed and send the bills to her.

Though he was privileged, Fred's childhood wasn't easy. He had severe asthma that kept him indoors during summer months, and he was often bullied. He struggled to fit in with his peers until high school. And it was these childhood experiences that inspired Fred's ministry to children.

In his biography of Fred, Maxwell King writes, "This was a pivotal theme of Rogers's life: from his earliest years, he took his fears, his loneliness and isolation, and his insecurities, and turned them to his advantage. Somehow, he was almost always able to take his feelings into a place of deep introspection and emerge with a fresh, and often brilliant, new direction. He did this as a child, as a high school student, and throughout his life, as a writer, an educator, and a television producer."

Fred's indelible impact on children and families is also the result of multiple difficult decisions that he made throughout his life. He could have chosen not to work at all, but instead he chose ministry. He left Dartmouth, an Ivy League school, to follow his heart and go to lesser-known Rollins College, a school more in line with his own identity and values. At Rollins, he met his wife and studied music composition, something that would later help to shape the programming of *Mister Rogers' Neighborhood*. After this, he was working at a major television network in New York and being groomed for a prominent role when he decided to move to Pittsburgh to work in educational television programming because he believed in it more.

"Fred Rogers took profound stock of his feelings to find meaning, often spiritual meaning, that he could turn into understanding, and eventually into the sort of serious focus that could yield power," explains King.

> *Question: How do I deal with my feelings?*
> *Prayer: Steady me.*

Am I being emotional or rational?
Is it an intuition or my intellect?
Am I wanting to do this out of fear or wisdom?

Do I want change because I am sad or because it's the right thing to do?
Am I acting out of anger or am I called to this?
Is it God or is it me?

These questions each contain a false binary when it comes to complex decisions that require deep change within us or in our circumstances.

There is something to be learned in both elements in each question, something needed from each part of what is coming up for us. And if you look at the longing behind each question, you will see we need both things, and we need them working together: feelings and reason, body and mind, heart and soul, you and God. God created you with all of these beautiful parts.

God can use each of these things, or all of them, to reach you, speak to you, empower you.

Some people think they should disregard their feelings and instead focus on "being rational" when making difficult decisions. This is a mistake for several reasons.

We can't choose between being rational and being emotional. Reason and feeling are caught up together within us. And our feelings are actually essential for making good decisions.

As adults, most of us wouldn't slap a friend that we are upset with because we don't want to feel shame and because we don't want our friend to feel violated. Similarly, we compliment people we want to be in relationship with because we want to feel accepted and accepting, loved and loving. We tell friends or close family members intimate details about our lives because we want to feel trusted and trusting. We explore possibilities with colleagues because we want to feel powerful and inspired. We share wins on social media because we desire to feel happy, successful, and respected.

Your feelings are also integral to social connection.

At the same time, you avoid doing some things because you don't want to experience difficult feelings. For example, we may say no to something that is beyond our capacity out of a desire to not feel stressed or scared. And sometimes we avoid doing things because we have learned that they incite difficult feelings in others. We don't cheat on our partner so they will not feel betrayed; we don't yell at our boss because we don't want to experience their disapproval.

Your feelings are important for guiding your intuitions (Will this make me feel fear or peace?), preferences (Am I disgusted by this or do I enjoy it?), interests (Do I feel passionate or apathetic about this?), motivation (Do I feel confident or discouraged while moving in this direction?), morality (Will this action make me feel guilty or joyful?), creativity (Am I feeling inadequate or daring?), beauty (Is this boring or fascinating?), and purpose (As I go toward this thing, do I feel more hopeless or more powerful?).

In Jesus's life, we see how feelings are connected to paying attention and living awake and aware. He wept at the sight of the city of Jerusalem and Mary in distress. He got angry and flipped tables. He was anxious in the Garden of Gethsemane. He felt abandoned on the cross.

You need your feelings on this journey. There are particular feelings that will be especially helpful to you during your decision-making journey.

For example, confusion is a great thing. Confusion fuels your desire to learn so you can figure out what to do. If you were not confused, you would have nothing to decide! Obviously too much confusion can lead to being overwhelmed and giving up. But you are avoiding being overwhelmed by reading this book.

The feeling of wonder will help you by inspiring your wish to understand your situation and how it is related to the larger reality of your life and the lives of others. "Wonder fuels our passion for exploration and learning, for curiosity and adventure," explains researcher and professor Brené Brown.

Curiosity and interest are two other powerful feelings for complex decision making by fueling your desire to ask questions, assess your beliefs and values, and "close the gap" between what you know and what you need to know to make your decision. Curiosity and interest motivate you to look for missing information. Also, feelings like these help you to engage your imagination and expand your vision. Awe is another helpful feeling on this journey. Awe can nurture humility and help you to value others more deeply, which impacts your desire to cooperate, share resources, and sacrifice for others—things that are often important in decision making.

*

Feelings are tricky though. When you express your feelings, be careful not to overidentify with them, saying things like, "I always have social anxiety." "I am a scaredy-cat." When we say these types of things, we can give feelings more meaning than they deserve.

We need to be able to separate our identity from how we feel. The difference between the two is "I am experiencing deep frustration" instead of "I am the angry person in my family." There is a "you" there beyond how you feel.

Difficult feelings can be obstacles to good decision making and incredibly harmful to you and others if you try and ignore them or uncritically give yourself over to them. And it's nearly impossible to figure out what to do when your mind is bogged down with difficult feelings. For example, it's hard to be wise about whether to stay or go if you feel betrayed or disappointed. Your feelings can get in the way of seeing anything beyond the hurt you are experiencing. I like to say some feelings are more difficult than others to feel, but no feeling is bad.

Don't make a decision impulsively because of a particular feeling related to a particular event. Quick, emotion-driven action can lead to regret. Your feelings are important information in your decision-making journey *and* there are other important kinds of information you are gathering.

It's easy to spend more time concentrating on how we think we should feel instead of accepting how we do feel, working through our emotions and learning from them.

*

Feelings are more conscious and more specific than emotions. Your body naturally has emotions, but your brain needs to become consciously aware of the feelings that flow from your emotions for your overall well-being.

Feelings are the meaning we make of emotions.

Our bodies react to our mental assessment of what is happening, so how we make meaning of our emotions and describe our feelings to ourselves and others *matters*.

These six E's of emotions can help you to acknowledge your emotions in a constructive way.

E-motion: Emotions are "energy in motion," as therapist Frida Rundell says. In order to get this energy out, first consider the question, where are you feeling this in your body? Are your shoulders tense? Do you feel this energy in your gut, in the center of your chest? Your lower back? Next, find a way to release this energy by grunting (if it is in your chest) or humming loudly (if it is in your gut), taking a stroll, or going for a run or swim. You could also move to upbeat music, cry, lift weights, do gentle stretches, get a massage, take deep breaths or take a bath or cold shower, or play an instrument.

Exact: Do your best to categorize and label what you are experiencing in as much detail as possible. What exactly are you feeling? Search for a feelings wheel online to help you. The more specific you are, the better you will respond to what is actually happening and the healthier you and your relationships and decisions will be. Also, the more exact you are about what feelings are coming up for you, the more accurately someone else can respond to you.

Express: Tell God what you are feeling. God listens to you and cares about what you are experiencing. Ask God to help you explore, evaluate, and examine your feelings.

Explore: As best you can, be an investigator and an observer. Picture the activating events in your mind. Imagine yourself as a fly on the wall seeing it all play out. Articulate to yourself what happened. When did this feeling begin? What triggered it?

Evaluate: Is there another way to look at what is happening, another way to tell the story? What is the most helpful or charitable way to think about the story or respond to it? Should you reach out to someone else and get a different perspective? Is this related to something that *just* happened or a past event? Are you experiencing the present through the past? Can the story be reframed? If not, simply move on to the next E, examine.

Examine: What insight can you gain?

Does something need to change?

Do you need something you can give yourself—rest; sleep; unplugging from texting, email, news, and social media platforms; exercise; a reset; a boundary; to say no?

Do you need to limit a substance that is causing your emotions to fluctuate: sugar, alcohol, other substances?

Do you need to articulate a want or need to someone else in a clear, kind way—an apology, equity, love, gentleness, patience, different communication, affirmation, something else?

Do you need to talk to a friend or therapist about what happened?

Do you need to work through your past? There is a chapter in this book, "Shedding," dedicated to reflecting on your past.

Your feelings can be helpful resources for determining what to do.
Your feelings are teachers. Allow them to signal to you what is good, what is wrong, and what needs to be attended to. For example, anger might indicate that something challenging or problematic has occurred that needs to be righted or processed.

Difficult feelings can be incredibly fruitful if you work through them with intentionality and grace for yourself and others. If you are currently experiencing difficult feelings, you need to first work through your feelings constructively in order to make room for insight, imagination, and clarity.

*

The following sections explore four difficult feelings: feeling numb, feeling frustrated or disgusted, feeling sad, and feeling afraid or anxious. If you know you are feeling one of these feelings now, you can go ahead and work through the section related to what you are feeling right now.

I encourage you to come back to this chapter whenever you are grappling with difficult feelings so you can work through them in constructive ways.

*

YOU FEEL NUMB

When tough things happen to you or around you, your mind and body can shut down. Sometimes things are so challenging that your brain can't comprehend what is occurring. You can tell you are moving through the world, but you feel disconnected from others and from yourself.

It is as if no one can make their way to you.

When you experience an acute traumatic event like the sudden death of a loved one or face chronic suffering (abuse, racism), your body can literally struggle to have energy or to react. You sort of go into a trance and block everything out. It's a protective mechanism.

If you are experiencing shock or dissociation, it will be difficult to respond to the rest of the invitations in this book.

If this is you, before jumping into the other aspects of this journey, I invite you to pay attention to your body, give it some love, and try a few things to get back in touch with yourself, with reality.

Set a small goal. Pick at least one thing to accomplish. A few ideas: Organize a drawer in your house while listening to music that moves you. Drink three glasses of water by the end of the day (not all at once). Write a thank-you or "I'm thinking of you" card and mail it. As we set and meet goals, we often feel alive again—even if it's a small feeling of success, interest, or optimism.

Even though it's very hard to want to move your body, I encourage you to get sunshine into your eyes right after waking and again at sunset. Just a few minutes of strolling your neighborhood (or a park) at the start *and* end of your day can help to calibrate your circadian rhythm, which will help you to sleep better and have more energy. Movement also impacts your brain and helps you have more pleasurable feelings.

Another thing that can be helpful is to set an appointment with a therapist, spiritual director, pastor or priest, or good friend. If you already meet with someone regularly, pick another category on this list and connect with someone else. You can do this online or in person. The idea is to create an opportunity to listen to someone else and be listened to. Listening and being heard help you to feel thankful, joyful, hopeful, valued, and energetic.

You might also seek inspiration in poetry, music, short stories, movies, and sacred texts. Allow yourself to be moved by what you read or hear, and afterward articulate to yourself the feelings rising up within you—whether they be enjoyable or difficult: shocked, hopeful, comforted.

This may seem like a wild idea if you feel apathetic, but it can also be incredibly helpful to find somewhere to volunteer.

I became a volunteer chaplain at a women's prison during the most difficult period of grief in my life (I write about this in my book *The Gravity of Joy*), and even though I felt like I had nothing to offer, it became a source of tremendous connection and healing in my life.

There are so many organizations in your community that need people's help.

You could volunteer to read with kids in an after-school program. You could become a friend to someone who has just moved to your city as a refugee. You could lead a group at a prison or coach a kid's sports team or do grassroots advocacy for a cause you believe in.

Serving other people nurtures feelings like joy, playfulness, interest, confidence, acceptance, trust, curiosity, and enthusiasm.

As you begin to set and accomplish small goals, take strolls, talk with people about what is going on in your life, or volunteer, the dam that is holding everything in will likely break open.

After you try something, write down or think through the feelings that are welling up within you. Choose one that is meaningful to you and *go through the six E's of emotions* as explained in the section above this one.

Eventually you will find yourself feeling again.

*

YOU FEEL FRUSTRATED OR DISGUSTED

Generally, you feel frustrated or disgusted because someone (maybe you) has done something that you believe is wrong. Usually this something violates a deeply held belief or value of yours. It often destroys your perspective of a person or organization. And feelings like anger and disappointment make it hard to think about anything else.

The six E's of emotion can be really helpful for figuring out why you are feeling the way you are feeling and what you can do about it.

E-motion: Where do you feel the frustration or disgust in your body? Can you give some extra care today to those places?

Do something with your feeling. If you feel the anger in your body, grab a kitchen towel or small bath towel and wring it between your two hands, twisting it and pulling it at the same time.

The action of dumping is also a very effective way of releasing difficult emotions related to frustration and disgust. Grab a notebook or journal that you do not mind ripping out pages of. You can always buy a cheap spiral notebook for this purpose. Get a pen and write what you are feeling and what is happening in you as fast and furiously as possible. Do not pay attention to grammar, spelling, or even the lines on the paper. Just get out everything you can think of as quickly as you can. Once you have written down everything you are feeling, rip out all the pages you have written on, crumple them up, and throw them away. Do not read what you have written or keep it. The idea is to *dump* your feelings.

You may want to build yourself a tool kit stocked with ways to calm yourself down: a candle, a comfy sweatshirt or lap blanket, a song list, a favorite tea. You could even design a peaceful place near a window. The idea is to use your calm-down tool kit when you feel angry to bring down your heart rate so you can actually explore, evaluate, and examine.

Exact: Get specific. If you feel *frustrated*, do you feel let down, humiliated, frustrated, bitter, distant, critical, dismissive, skeptical, aggressive, withdrawn, annoyed, infuriated, provoked, jealous, furious, violated, offended, ridiculed, disrespected, resentful, betrayed?

If you feel *disgusted*, do you feel disapproving, disappointed, awful, repelled, hesitant, horrified, nauseated, revolted, appalled, embarrassed, judgmental? See the feelings wheel.

Express: Tell God exactly what you are feeling. Ask God any questions you have. The Psalms are full of frustration and disgust. God can handle your anger and any other difficult feeling you experience. Ask God to help you explore, evaluate, and examine your feelings so you can move through them in a helpful way.

God expects your anger, especially when something wrong happens. God isn't too small for your frustration or disgust. God can handle your difficult feelings. Throughout the Bible, people who loved God passionately got passionately disturbed. As we pray through how we are feeling, God shows up. You can feel God comforting you, supporting you, being present to you. You can sense God guiding you toward what is next.

Explore: As best you can, be an investigator and an observer. Picture yourself when you initially felt anger or disgust rising up within you. What was the triggering event? Was it something someone did or said? Tell the story of what happened. You could write it out in a journal or draw a picture or create a voice memo for yourself in your smart phone.

Evaluate: It's very difficult to reframe what has happened when you feel disgusted or frustrated. Once you have dumped your emotions, though, you might be able to talk to a friend, mentor, therapist, or spiritual director and get some perspective. Is there more to the story? What woundedness or baggage led to the wrong that occurred? Is it possible to transform your feelings by opening yourself to empathy for yourself, someone else, or an organization? What would it take to live a new story?

Examine: Finally, is there anything you have learned from this situation and these difficult feelings? And, what do you need to move forward into the future? Articulate exactly what you need to let this go. It could be that you need a significant boundary or a major shift in a relationship or intentional work on communication or a habit adjustment. What do you need? What needs to change? People can't read our minds. Ask for what you need and see if it can be given. At the very least, is there some kind of compromise that can be reached?

*

YOU FEEL SAD

There are many reasons you could feel sad during your decision-making journey. Big decisions usually involve loss or change, and both can cause feelings of sadness and related feelings.

Perhaps you have heard words that really hurt you, or you feel like you have no good choices regarding your decision, only tough ones.

You might also feel sad if you have done something you regret or if you are considering a big transition that will impact where you live, how you spend your time, how much money you make. Maybe your health has changed and you feel powerless.

There are many forms of sadness. It is one thing to feel lonely, and an entirely different thing to feel ashamed. Use the six E's of emotions to describe what you are feeling.

E-motion: Where do you feel the sadness in your body? Can you give some extra care today to those places?

Do some gentle stretches and then massage your hands and feet. Use your fingers to massage your palms and the arches and heels of your feet.

Exact: Be as specific as possible. Do you feel hurt, guilty, desperate, vulnerable, lonely, embarrassed, disappointed, inferior, empty, remorseful, powerless, fragile, victimized, abandoned?

Express: God truly cares about your sadness. God sees you. God is a witness to your sadness and is with you in your sadness. Your sadness is not too much for God. You can be honest about anything you are feeling with God, and as you share what you are feeling with God, your burden will be eased. You will feel lighter if you share it and give some of your sadness away. God will help you to move through your sadness rather than avoid it.

When you weep, God sees your tears. When you can't get out of bed and struggle to keep going, God is near to you. God hears your stress, your cries for help, your anguish, and your desire for things to be different, to feel different, for life to be good again.

Spend about twenty minutes writing your own lament. A lament is your own version of a letter, poem, song.

Laments are addressed to God. Lament is a form of protest. Lament is also a way to process emotion. Lament gives us a place to voice confusion.

Lament draws attention to injustice and suffering and asks God to do something about it.

Drawing on both the model of the Psalms in the Old Testament and religious educator Anne Streaty Wimberly's edited volume *From Lament to Advocacy*, we can outline the practice of lament as follows:

1. Naming—State openly and honestly what makes you feel the way you do.
2. Questioning—Write down all your questions and confusions. Where are you, God? Why didn't you show up?
3. Imagining—Imagine what could happen next. If God were to break into your situation, what might God do? Who have you known God to be? What is God like? What might be possible in light of who God is?

Explore: As best you can, be an investigator and an observer. Draw a picture of your sadness. What color is it? How big is it? How much does it weigh? What shape does it take? Is it more within you or something outside of you that follows you or walks with you? Something else?

Evaluate: It isn't always possible to reframe what is happening, but sometimes we can see our sadness in new ways by thinking about it from someone else's perspective, zooming out and thinking about the bigger picture (seeing our sadness as just one part of our story), or reconsidering it all together. Perhaps you have more agency than you first realized. Or maybe your mind told you one story and it wasn't a helpful story or the full story, and you need to tell yourself a different story.

Examine: Do you need something you can give yourself—rest; sleep; unplugging from texting, email, news, and social media platforms; exercise; a reset; a boundary; to say no? Do you need to articulate a want or need to someone else in a clear, kind way—an apology, equity, love, gentleness, patience, different communication, affirmation, something else? Do you need to talk to a friend or therapist or spiritual director?

＊

YOU FEEL AFRAID OR ANXIOUS

Big decisions cause us to feel fearful or anxious for many reasons. Perhaps you already made a decision that you now believe was a bad decision, and you don't trust yourself to make good decisions anymore.

Perhaps you feel fearful or anxious because change terrifies you. We tend to resist change even if the status quo kills our spirit. But change is inevitable. It's baked into the universe, conversion, and the spiritual life.

You change all the time. Think about it. How have you changed in the last ten years, in the last year? And what change have you been capable of?

Your fears or anxiety could also come from a desire to not want to feel rejection, loneliness, or vulnerability. Perhaps you fear the unknown. If your future feels uncertain or you don't know the long-term consequences of what you are considering, you may feel fearful or anxious about what could happen. You may feel overwhelmed by what-ifs.

Fear about a difficult decision is rarely about an actual threat. If yours is, I urge you to contact a domestic violence center in your community or some other type of group that can help you, depending on who is causing you to feel afraid.

More often, fear or anxiety is related to an imagined threat, negative thought patterns, worst-case-scenario thinking, or feeling out of control or disconnected.

E-motion: In a moment of feeling flooded by fear or anxiety, it's impossible to think clearly. Often our mind shuts down and the world gets blurry. In these moments, we need to ground ourselves.

Here are four ways to do this:

1. Engage Your Senses: Look around you and find five things you can see. Now, find four things you can touch and touch them.

Listen. Are there three things you can hear? Smell. Are there two things you can smell? Finally, taste. Run your tongue across the roof of your mouth. Can you taste one thing?

2. Try Box Breathing. Breathe in for four counts. Hold for four counts. Breathe out for four counts. Hold for four counts. Do this four times.

3. Do a Body Scan. Find a comfortable position and close your eyes. Scan your entire body starting with your toes. Literally imagine each body part in your mind as you say it to yourself. Toes. Heels. Top of feet. Ankles. Calves. Right knee. Left knee. Thighs. Hips. Lower back. Upper back. Stomach. Chest. Shoulders. Arms. Right hand. Left hand. Neck. Chin. Nose. Eyes. Cheeks. Right ear. Left ear. Forehead. Face. Entire body. I am here. I am still here.

4. Imagine your entire body being held by God's embrace. Imagine being held, guided. Imagine natural settings that are beautiful. Imagine people being good to you. Challenge any negative thoughts with helpful, loving thoughts. I am capable. I am loved. I am brave.

"Fear is an energy that restrains us . . . love, on the other hand expands us," explains theologian John Chryssavgis.

These are all grounding practices that can bring immediate calm during a moment of anxiety or fear.

You and your family members can use these practices when you are scared, worried, taking a test, about to speak in front of people, fighting with each other, panicking about the future, or feeling stressed.

Exact: Characterize your emotion in detail. Do you feel scared, weak, insecure, rejected, threatened, exposed, nervous, persecuted, excluded, insignificant, worthless, inferior, inadequate, worried, overwhelmed, frightened, helpless?

Don't overidentify with your fear or anxiety by deciding you are just a fearful or anxious person. This could look like telling people, "I am always scared when . . ." or "I always have anxiety." You aren't the fearful, anxious person. Instead, your mind is telling you a story about why you need to feel afraid or anxious.

Express: Jesus says two things most often during his ministry. "Follow me" and "Do not be afraid." God doesn't want you to live in fear or to be paralyzed by your anxiety. God wants you to feel a deep sense of peace.

How has God been faithful to you? My mom often reminds me of this when I fear the future. She tells me what God has done for me in the past, how God has taken care of me. Perhaps recall how you have been taken care of. When did you need help and help arrived?

Offer your fears and anxieties to God. Ask God to help you explore, evaluate, and examine them.

Explore: General fear or anxiety is related to your perception of what is currently happening. It's based on how you have assessed the situation you are in or the state of your life. And with God's love and the help of others, challenging thoughts can be worked through. Where is your current fear or anxiety coming from? Is there an actual problem? If there is, what might you do to solve it? If your fear or anxiety is from something that *could* go wrong, recognize that this is currently an imagined problem rather than an actual problem.

Evaluate: We often think of "what-ifs" that are negative, harmful, or terrible. Instead, imagine positive what-ifs. What would be the best possible scenario?

What if everything is going to be all right?

Ask yourself: What if this is exactly what I am hoping for? What if I do this with confidence? What if I can trust myself? What if people are happy for me? What if this brings me peace? What if I get more rest? What if this change helps me live more abundantly? What if this is the best thing that has ever happened to me?

Recognize that what is unknown may actually be good!

Examine: Finally, what might you gain from understanding your fear or anxiety more deeply? What do these emotions or what you are going through teach you about what you value, believe, desire, or need?

Embedded in a fear is often a desire. We fear failure because we desire success or goodness (or other positive things). We fear rejection because we desire connection and love. We fear making the wrong decision because we desire a beautiful life.

What is the desire behind your fear? Is this a helpful desire, something good for you and worthy of who you are? If so, what does it take to pursue it? Perhaps your journey is more about determining the habits, beliefs, values, and shifts that will support this desire. Maybe you need the help of others too.

Do you need to ask for something you need? Do you need to nurture yourself in some way?

FIELD NOTES TO SELF

- Your feelings are an essential part of this journey.
- Difficult feelings can become obstacles to good decision making if you ignore them.
- The six E's of emotion can help you work through difficult feelings.

SUMMONING

When You Are Struggling to Imagine the Future

Who loved you into being?

—Patrick B. Reyes, *The Purpose Gap*

As she tried to teach the elementary-school students in Stockton, California, Dolores grew more and more saddened. She knew they were too hungry and too exhausted to learn. Her students, most of whom were farmworkers' children, showed up to class malnourished, in tattered clothes and shoes, sometimes with no shoes on at all.

The more she reflected on what she could do for these children, the more she realized she could only truly help them if she advocated for their caregivers to have improved working and living conditions.

At the time, farmworkers were the worst-paid workers in the United States. During their long work hours when it was often over 100 degrees, they were given little to no water and no access to restrooms. Rape and other forms of brutal treatment were also common. The families of farmworkers were living in crowded and cramped shacks, tents, abandoned buildings, and converted buses and chicken coops. The places where they stayed were unsanitary, dilapidated, and especially unsuitable for children.

When farmworkers would try to advocate for themselves, they experienced discrimination and violence. Dolores believed that the system they worked within was degrading and humiliating and was even worse than the daily backbreaking labor.

Dolores wanted to commit her life to volunteer work, activism, and communal support in an effort to create better working conditions.

Yet doing so would mean changing every aspect of her life. It would mean moving to a small town without knowing how she would pay her bills. And it would impact not just her life but also the lives of her seven children. And to make matters more difficult, she was in the middle of a divorce.

Question: Who am I?
Prayer: Inspire me.

There are gems buried in the stories that have made us. We can reflect on the stories that give shape to our identities and find our values, convictions, and gifts.

Most of the boldest choices I have made in my life were possible by summoning up parts of my story and the stories of my community and faith that my life is held within.

Another step in this journey toward figuring out what to do is for you to reclaim.

You carry within you a resounding yes. There is something there that burns, that fuels you. It gives you life whether you have realized this or not.

What is your resounding yes? Is it a value, a gift, a dream, a hope? It's usually related to your *why*, your reason for getting out of bed every morning.

And who lit this flame within you?

If you are unclear on the yes within you, stay with me. It may be forgotten, or perhaps it has been suppressed by the many competing demands on your life.

Thinking about the stories that make us helps us to know more about who we are. There is wisdom in the stories that have shaped us. In her memoir, the poet Joy Harjo writes, "I was entrusted with carrying voices, songs, and stories to grow and release into the world, to be of assistance and inspiration. These were my responsibility. I am not special. It is this way for everyone. We enter into a family story, and then other stories based on tribal towns and nations, lands, countries, planetary systems, and universes. Yet we each have our own individual story to tend."

Your story is important, and it is connected to and born from the stories of people, living and dead, that have loved you into existence, given you life, fought for life.

*

Dolores eventually made the huge, incredibly difficult decision to leave her job and comfortable home in Stockton to move to a small town, Delano, not knowing where her next meal would be coming from.

Many people thought she was making a very foolish decision. Even her own family didn't understand why she would give up everything to work with farmworkers who had nothing.

Yet she felt her calling strongly.

Speaking about her mother, Dolores's daughter Juana explains, "César Chavez and my mother were both greatly influenced by the philosophies of Gandhi. You can't help people unless you live like them."

Dolores prayed for a sign that she was going in the wrong direction, a sign that never came.

Instead, the day after she made the decision to quit her job and move, groceries showed up on her front porch. She took this instead as a positive sign that she was going in the right direction and that she and her children would be taken care of as long as she stayed committed to her calling.

Dolores talks about her desire to pass on her passion for helping others to her children, explaining, "We have a tendency to want to be too comfortable, and I'm trying to educate my children in the way that I am raising them to give their lives to work for other people."

Both Dolores and her children gave up a lot—safety, especially. Her kids were shot at, spent time in labor camps with her, and lived at people's homes without her when she was leading rallies and protests and traveling to connect with political leaders and change laws.

Dolores was also jailed twenty-two times, and even though Chavez and Huerta were committed to nonviolence (and always protested nonviolently), she nearly died at one point after being beaten severely by police at a public demonstration.

Taking a peek into Dolores Huerta's family and history provides some insight into what contributed to her sense of call and the courage to remain committed to it.

Dolores's grandfather watched her a lot when she was growing up. He gave her the nickname "Seven Tongues," since she talked a lot, and he always encouraged her to speak her mind and argue for what she believed in.

Her mom treated Dolores like she treated her sons, equally. Her mother encouraged her to go to college, and even though she was the only Chicana in her classes and experienced discrimination, she remained in school and did well because of her family's support.

Dolores's mother owned several businesses during her lifetime; one was a hotel. With compassion, she often offered laborers who were poor rooms for one dollar or for no money at all. Dolores was a witness to her mother's concern for people who are underresourced.

Dolores's response to the call on her life was a kind of summoning.

She recovered how she was raised and retrieved her identity as a powerful woman who could use her voice to create meaningful change and show compassion for people who are poor and mistreated.

Dolores Huerta is among the most important activists in American history. She was an equal partner in cofounding and coleading the first farmworkers union with César Chavez and has spent her life advocating for people and teaching people to advocate for themselves.

Huerta and Chavez eventually organized workers and allies across the states and were able to gain higher wages and more respectful treatment of workers, including the end of growers spraying pesticides while farmworkers were in the fields.

When Dolores was interviewed in a documentary about her life about why she has been willing to make such difficult decisions, she responded, "This is my life's work. To me, this is the reason I live."

*

As I think about the choices I have made throughout my own life, many of them quite bold, I can also look at my family and understand why. When I was fifteen, I told my mom I wanted to live in the Upper Peninsula of Michigan for the summer, working at Lake Ellen Bible Camp.

I had a deep conviction about going there to work for the summer cleaning bathrooms, connecting with others, and communing with God among the trees. What is kind of wild, though, is, I had never been to this camp. And I didn't know anyone who worked there. I had never even been to Michigan. Plus, this was several years before I had a cell phone.

I don't remember exactly what Mom said, but I know that she wholeheartedly supported my decision. Her questions were mainly related to logistics and how she could help me to do what I felt called to do.

Neither my wild idea or her generous support of it was out of the ordinary. All of my life Mom has taught me to pray, listen for God's guidance, trust it, and follow God's voice toward any big idea I have felt God was asking me to attend to.

As I look back, all I have ever dreamed of doing, Mom has supported. She's never been one to question my hopes or to give me reasons things won't work out or can't happen. Instead, she's always been the person who, with excitement, has said some version of "That will be wonderful. I'm overjoyed with you. I look forward to hearing what happens."

To this day, she is my favorite person to tell when something wonderful happens.

Not only this, but my mom was the primary person who raised me growing up. From seven years old, I have watched her as a single mother trust God and keep moving forward when she had little to no money in her bank account, when she had to reinvent herself and find a sustainable career, and when she had to move across the state with two small children, all while managing her health. I have seen her lean on God again and again and never feel failed.

Her faith, her strength, her trust in God lives in me.

Because of the many stories I carry within about sharing possibilities, pathways, and visions with my mom and getting unwavering support, I walk through life trusting God and myself to be able to walk toward anything I feel called to with confidence.

Whenever I get worried about the future or can't quite imagine the future, I try to draw upon what has been passed on to me.

My mom has four sisters, and my grandmother was the matriarch of the family, who was a vibrant presence in all of our lives. All the women in my family, including mamaw, have or have had careers with high demands. There is an expectation in my family that women courageously go after their dreams, embrace their power as human beings, and create a life for themselves that they can be proud of.

This story in my family far outshined any story about the "place of women" that might say otherwise. Similarly, there has been a consistent theme in my family of making something of what has been given to you. Take what you have and multiply it. Do better for the next generation.

Summon up the meaningful family stories that you have inherited. Perhaps they are stories about ancestors, matriarchs and patriarchs, tall tales, mysteries. Maybe particular historical events greatly impacted your family. What happened? What themes emerge when you think about what kind of family you come from?

If you are adopted or grew up living with different adults, consider the stories of your childhood. What does it mean to you now? What kind of person did your experiences shape you to be? What are the values or virtues that these stories teach you?

Within you there is a well.

It has been filled by those who loved you and also by those who have come before you—ancestors and a community you were born into that has navigated suffering, struggled to live awake, and been witnesses to the world's beauty, goodness, and meaning.

I haven't lived in Kentucky for twenty years, but Kentucky lives in me.

When I consider my cultural heritage, I think of how Kentuckians are quite oriented toward community. We feel obligations to care for our people deeply. For many Kentuckians, family is family, no matter how distant the relative. We come together in hard times. Tradition and ritual are important too. Watching a horse race or a basketball game is not simply a fun activity; it is a way of gathering, of celebrating, of enjoying life together in the midst of hard work, financial instability, pain and struggle.

For many Kentuckians, church is also woven into the fabric of community life. It's how you make friends and have other people to eat with and help you fix your roof.

The places you have lived have made and formed you too. You carry the stories of those places, and their cultural traditions and rituals impact how you live.

Often the stories we carry within us have themes that can anchor us or be like guiding stars as we move through life.

As you consider the stories that have made you, what inspires you? What needs summoning?

*

During a conference for educators who teach various forms of youth ministry, invited speaker Anne Streaty Wimberly shared an inspiring story. Dr. Anne, as she is affectionately called, is a religious educator and author. In her eighties on stage, she reflected on turning thirteen.

When a person turned thirteen in her church, they were brought to the front during a worship service to be celebrated. When it was Dr. Anne's turn, elders in the church stood next to her in front of the congregation and told her the gifts they saw in her. They told her they had loved to watch her become who she was and that they looked forward to the ways she would use her gifts in the community.

In this moment on stage decades later, she could still recall much of what they shared with her. Those adults spoke words of life to her. *They affirmed who she was and said her life mattered in the community.*

Maybe you haven't experienced what Dr. Anne has, but you have likely had at least one person who has *loved you into being.* Think back. Trace your life. Think about your mentors, teachers, coaches, family members, friends, coworkers. Who has loved you to life? Who has named truths in you?

As my friend Patrick Reyes's grandma taught him, there is wisdom in the words and faces of people who have loved you into being.

If you are struggling to remember or if you simply could use some encouragement, text at least one person you know well and ask them to tell you the truth about yourself.

Once, I was having a terrible day where I could feel myself telling myself terrible things about who I was. I texted seven people (so, yes, you can text seven people if you want!) and said, "I am having a bad day. I need someone to tell me the truth about myself. What do you know to be true about me?"

I was hoping one or two people would get back to me with words that would reconnect me to myself. To my surprise, within an hour, all of them wrote me back, and their loving words called me out of my negativity and deep sadness.

Similarly, when I was trying to figure out what to do regarding work, I interviewed several people who know me well from various aspects of my life using questions from entrepreneur John Berardi's book *Changemaker.* Not only was it an incredibly encouraging experience, it was illuminating. It helped me to understand what I do naturally (and most of the time not consciously) as well as some of my limitations.

I encourage you to interview at least three people who know you well, asking the following questions (text, phone call, email, in person all work). These are a mixture of my own questions and Berardi's questions.

1. How would you describe me? What are my talents, abilities, and characteristics?
2. What makes me come alive?
3. How would you describe my way of doing things?
4. What do you count on me for?

I was surprised not only to learn more about my strengths but also to learn about my liabilities and limits. "We are led to truth by our weaknesses as well as our strengths," writes speaker and activist Parker Palmer.

I found these interviews to be incredibly clarifying and inspiring. Some of what was shared were new ways of understanding myself.

Encouragement has the word "courage" in it. When we are encouraged by people who care about us, we become braver. We remember how capable we are, and their truth-telling becomes a kind of launchpad for us.

*

Some of us have experienced such beautiful times in our lives that we can't look forward and imagine life could get any better. We glorify what was, dwell in it, and relive it constantly. We wonder, can there be life after an amazing career, peak performance in a favorite sport, a brilliant relationship with a deceased spouse?

Your incredible experience was composed of multiple meaningful elements. And you can take these elements—values, beliefs, actions—and integrate them into a new story.

If your work involved leadership, mentorship, and deep connections with people, you could join Big Brothers, Big Sisters and mentor a young person who could use your wisdom, guidance, and care.

If you were an incredible athlete, take the work ethic, dedication, and love you had and put it toward learning something new—cooking for people, playing pickleball with aging neighbors, running marathons for a charity.

You can summon up the threads of the best—moment, experience, relationship, year of your life—and take what you loved and let it feed the future. If you would like to spend time reflecting on some of the most meaningful moments in your life, there is an activity in the appendix related to this chapter that will help you.

*

Mary McLeod Bethune was born in 1875 to former slaves in Mayesville, South Carolina. The midwife who helped birth her said she was born with her eyes wide open, and, true to her birth day, she spent her life this way.

She spent some of her earliest years, before the age of seven, picking cotton twelve hours a day. There were no schools for children who were Black.

A pivotal moment in her young life was when she picked up a book at the home of a white family and one of the members told her to get a picture book instead. She immediately had a *burning desire* to read and became determined to be educated.

When she was seven, a woman opened up a school and wanted Mary to attend, and though her family needed her working in the fields, her parents eventually allowed her to go once Mary convinced her father. She walked five miles to and from school.

Mary never took her education for granted.

She was known for her deep faith in herself and God. Throughout her life, she often spoke of three dreams she had had that encouraged and motivated her.

In one dream, she stood on a riverbank wondering how to get across and saw an army of young people behind her. She was told by someone to register the names of all the young people in the group into a book before crossing.

After this dream, she began to sense God was inviting her to help other kids like her to read and get an education. She held on to this dream and allowed it to be a guiding vision.

Her second dream placed her on the banks of this same river. She was helped some of the way across by her parents and some of the way by a leader of an institution but needed to figure out how to find the rest of the way across.

Between these two dreams, she felt that she had been prepared for a life of service and was confident she had a purpose she needed to fulfill, specifically to build a school for children like her.

Her third dream put her on the bank of a different river. In the dream, she was praying for a way to build a school when Booker T. Washington jumped off a horse and handed her a diamond from his handkerchief. "Take this and build your school," he told her. She had read about him but hadn't met him in real life. When she woke up, she felt the diamond represented all that was necessary from her life for building her school: confidence, willpower, stick-to-it-iveness, work, suffering, friends, doubt, wisdom, common sense.

Mary's summoning was a kind of gathering of all that she had gained and experienced.

She started a school with $1.50 and five little girls that over time became a thriving accredited college. She went on to cultivate relationships with the most influential politicians and activists of her day—specifically working to improve the lives of African Americans.

When she died in 1955, she was considered one of the most influential and greatest women of the twentieth century.

Your dreams have treasures. If you reflect on them, you can recover hopes, values, inspiration, motivation, a picture of what is worth wanting.

Some questions for reflecting on your dreams:

- What feelings did you experience throughout the dream?
- If you're experiencing any of these feelings when you're awake, what might this mean?
- Who was present in the dream? What do they represent for you?

- When you think about current life events in light of the dream, what is revealed to you?

*

Here is an important story you might need to summon up: *God made you good.*

This is the shared truth at the very beginning of the Bible. God made the world, including humans, and called all of it good.

Yes, you.

God isn't twiddling God's thumbs wondering when you will earn God's favor. God isn't sighing deeply, wondering whether you will become kinder, more grateful, more worthy of God's guidance and blessings. God isn't some kind of a frustrated parent hiding in the back bedroom trying to cool off before talking to you again.

God is reaching out to you, right now, just as you are. Right in the middle of the paragraph you are living, you are loved unconditionally. Full stop. No matter what decisions or transitions you have made or will make.

I love the wisdom of Solomon. He describes God writing, "You love everything that exists. You despise nothing that you made. If you hated it, you wouldn't have created it. Nothing could survive unless you willed it. Nothing could remain unless you continued to call into being. You spare all things because all things are yours, ruler and lover of life."

We forget sometimes, but Genesis 1 wins. God wins. Good wins.

You and me, we are also a part of the Great Story being told. We participate in this story.

This is the story that mysteriously says,

> God loves everything,
> and made it all good,
> everyone belongs,
> all is being restored,
> *and resurrection,*

not death
always, always gets the last word.

Summon up the truth about who you are and your place in God's story.

God's story doesn't rely on any one decision we make.

If you take a wrong turn, there is grace. There is unconditional love. There is enough. Your life is still held within the Great Story.

If we let them, spiritual stories about us and the world being made good, about God's unconditional love, and about our ability to participate in God's story can orient us.

- What religious and spiritual stories have fed your soul?
- What are the major themes or ideas of these stories, and are they true?
- What parts of these stories do you want to cling to during this decision-making journey?

Spiritual experiences nourish our souls too.

Lisa Miller is a clinical psychologist and scientist. She studies the relationship between psychology and spirituality. She has been able to show through brain mapping that everyone has a spiritual center in their brain, which means you have a "spiritual self" that is one-third nature and two-thirds nurture.

Her research has proven empirically that when the spiritual core is strengthened, people have less severe depressive episodes and their episodes are shorter and they are also less suicidal.

Spiritual attunement is a *protective factor* against depression and despair.

Not only this, but Miller and her team have found that spiritual experiences change the physicality of our brains in healthy ways. In one of their studies, Miller and her team recorded the brain activity of young adults as they first told a story about a stressful event, and then one about a spiritual experience.

While talking about the stressful event, the brain's frontal lobe would light up. This is the part responsible for motivation and reward. Miller noticed that all the stories involved working very hard to gain control over an uncertain situation.

Stress activates what she calls "the achieving mind," a mode of awareness that focuses on organizing and controlling our lives. The achieving mind asks, "How can I get and keep the things I want in life?" Which feels to me like a very legitimate question.

I can relate with the achieving mind. I feel like this is my brain times ten when I am trying to maintain what I think I need or want and keeping too many plates spinning because I can't bear to imagine letting anything break.

Maybe I would break.

In contrast, during Miller's research studies, *telling a spiritual experience* activated different parts of the participants' brains: the part associated with love and another portion, where we experience feelings of unity and belonging, as well as the part of our brain where we see the world as active and speaking to us. Your spiritual experiences don't have to be miraculous, ecstatic, or bizarre to be incredibly meaningful. In fact, most happen during ordinary moments on ordinary days.

There have been multiple times I have experienced significant God moments in my life, but perhaps one of the most enlightening ones happened in middle school.

I was in Gatlinburg, Tennessee, at a church conference for young people. Surrounded by friends, I was singing with my eyes closed and my hands in the air. Suddenly, I saw an image of Jesus in front of me.

Jesus walked through me and I sensed God saying to me, "Be my hands and feet in the world."

To this day, I have never had another mystical spiritual experience quite like this one (it is the most mysterious of my life). Instantly, it felt as if God had given me a sacred invitation to invest in others through teaching, preaching, and speaking.

It didn't make much sense as a seventh grader in speech therapy. I had a speech impediment that made it very difficult for people to understand me. In fact, my part in a school play was taken away a couple of years before this due to the directors feeling like the audience would not understand what I was saying.

Yet I felt God would show me the way over time.

Initially, this beautiful, compelling invitation from God was affirmed by my youth pastor Dale. Right after I told him what happened, he said I should lead youth group. This wasn't a small task since about one hundred kids came regularly to youth group.

A few months later, I did.

Then in tenth grade, I tried explaining my holy experience and the call on my life to a new youth leader who, in contrast to Dale, said I could be the wife of a pastor but couldn't be one myself. This is a common refrain among the Southern Baptist Christians I grew up with, people telling women they must have heard God incorrectly, people telling women that God has called them to marriage and to support someone else's call to ministry instead.

Here's the thing: I couldn't unhear what I'd heard in seventh grade. It was cemented in my soul. I couldn't unsee what I had seen. It was a part of me. And thankfully, Dale had already confirmed and supported what I had heard. So, I found a new church and held on to the experience I had in middle school.

Again, in college, someone questioned this call on my life. I was attending Oklahoma Baptist University, and the dean of theology found me after chapel one day specifically to talk to me about preaching in class earlier that week. During class, the professor put the students into small groups. Each group was supposed to choose a member to preach, and my group chose me.

The dean must have been told about the class from students who were unhappy that women were chosen to preach. "Men preach, women teach," the dean insisted. And with no opportunity for me to respond, he walked away. It was a monologue, not a dialogue.

I still couldn't unhear what I had heard. I couldn't unsee what I'd seen in middle school. The dean's words were low static in the background of a vivid, extravagant song God was playing in the world, a song that had captured my heart long ago. That holy pause where I stopped and listened, that encounter with God as a nervous, hormonal teen stumbling my way through middle school has sustained me on many days in my life. We carry encounters with the living God within us, and those encounters carry us.

There have been moments in your life when you knew who you were. Even if they feel like distant memories right now, even if you feel like what you have to work with is scraps, you can summon from your communal and family stories, from the people who have loved you, from that best time in your life, from your dreams and your spiritual stories and experiences and name possibilities and pathways forward.

- What story, story line about yourself/your community might you resurrect today?
- And from your summoning, what possibilities and pathways are emerging?

FIELD NOTES TO SELF

- Recall to mind the faces of the people who have loved you into being.
- Recover what's worth wanting by remembering a dream or other type of spiritual experience you've had.
- Resurrect a story line that gives you strength.

SHEDDING

When Your Past Weighs on You

We don't give enough glory to exodus.
In any new life season, you can't make
a big entrance without a really glorious exit.
Want love? Leave rooms where you're not called beloved.
Want purpose? Abandon what feels meaningless.
Want inspiration? Forsake that which doesn't feed you.
For millennia, every green thing in the natural
world has taught us this.
There is no radiance
without first a rupture.

—Joy Sullivan

Rachel Held Evans was an author, a blogger, and, for countless people, a spiritual guide. She died at the relatively young age of thirty-seven due to an allergic reaction to medication for an infection that caused swelling in her brain.

Laura Jean Truman captures her enormous influence when she writes, "Rachel was our pastor, but our church didn't have a building that we can go to to be together. She gathered strangers on her Twitter feed and made us family, and I don't know where else to mourn now except on this screen with all our people."

Rachel was known for her ability to articulate beautifully the human experience and especially what it feels like to wrestle with one's faith and the communities that formed it. In her book *Searching for Sunday*, Rachel shares her decision to leave a church community that had been like family.

She spent her high school years attending Grace Bible Church and loved it. So, later, when she got married to her husband, Dan, and they moved back to her hometown, the couple began attending it together.

Over time, Rachel began to struggle with what she was hearing during worship services. "On Sunday mornings, my doubt came to church like a third member of the family, toddling along behind me with clenched fists and disheveled hair, throwing wild tantrums after every offhanded political joke and casual reference to hell," she recalls.

Rachel had multiple contending convictions that were taken for granted and serious questions while others nodded around her during Sunday services. To make matters worse, she writes, "I was surrounded by the people who knew, and loved me best in the world, and yet it was the loneliest hour of my week. I felt like an interloper, a fake."

Pressured by this loneliness, Rachel slowly checked out, first in spirit and then in body. Looking back, she wished she had not remained silent about her beliefs and questions, but rather had talked with other congregants and leaders about what she was thinking and feeling. Rachel wondered if her church could have loved her through disagreement.

In order to work through what was happening within her, she began blogging about her doubt and questioning of her church's position on a number of issues including sexuality and gender roles. Many people responded to her blogs with a version of "me too." But neighbors and former fellow parishioners started gossiping about her, whispering that she had become a Buddhist, which wasn't true. To his credit, instead of joining the gossip, Rachel's former pastor asked to talk to the couple.

During the conversation, Rachel and Dan focused on the church's statement of beliefs and explained why they no longer agreed with many of its points. At the end of the conversation, the pastor thanked them for all they had done for the church through their service over the years. As they walked out of the doors of the church, they felt like they had done the right thing, and yet their sadness was palpable. Once they got into their car and shut the door, Rachel writes, "I put my head in my hands and cried, startled to tears by the selfishness of my own thoughts, *'Who will bring us casseroles when we have a baby?'*"

Throughout *Searching for Sunday*, Rachel explores the various Christian communities that shaped her by telling stories about seven sacraments of the church, starting with baptism and ending with marriage. While she did find other churches to attend, she says the book is not about finding a Sunday church but instead is about searching for Sunday resurrection.

Question: Why can't I move forward?
Prayer: Relieve me.

Philosopher and mystic Meister Eckhart points out that the spiritual life is more about subtraction than about addition.

When I first read this, I thought, "Lord, have mercy. How have I missed this? How have I lived so much of my life the other way around?"

When Jesus talks about losing our life to find it, he seems to mean we die regularly *as we live*. A good life doesn't avoid death. It accepts death, even welcomes it, knowing that death in all its forms—death of the way things have been and the way I wanted them to be, death of dreams, beliefs, fears, versions of my self, relationships, people—is necessary for resurrection, restoration, wholeness, love.

Jesus gave us a profound metaphor when he called himself "the vine" and his followers "branches." And in order to bear good fruit, God the gardener clips and trims branches.

It is the cutting back that mysteriously nurtures growth.

Shedding creates the conditions for something new to come forth.

Joy Sullivan writes compellingly about the necessity of exodus and rupture in the poem that opened this chapter. Sometimes we need to depart in order to enter the new. Sometimes we need to break on the way to wholeness. Sometimes, as in the work of chemotherapy, healing comes through destruction. Sometimes we relinquish what we know to gain new insight.

As John Chryssavgis put it, the beautiful thing is "when we learn what to let go of, we also learn what it is that is worth holding on to."

*

In order to keep moving forward, you may need to shed betrayal or disappointment and forgive a person or an organization that has hurt you.

"Forgiveness is a process that comes in droplets," theologian Miroslav Volf says. I take this to mean we give a little of it at first. Then we give it again, maybe a bit more. We do one step at a time, until over time, we have offered the situation to God and no longer ruminate on it.

Forgiveness is akin to mercy.

We release the person to God though they do not deserve it, have not earned it, and the situation is unfair. As we engage the process of forgiveness, we remember the event(s) in new ways and do our best to let go of resentment.

Forgiveness does not mean you give this person permission to hurt you again.

Forgiveness is different from repentance, justice, and reconciliation. It doesn't require an apology. You can offer forgiveness to someone who isn't sorry. Justice can follow or be paired with forgiveness, but it is different. Justice requires some kind of repair or reparations. And forgiveness doesn't necessarily mean you renew the relationship.

Forgiveness is your gift to someone else that mirrors God's forgiveness to you—that unconditional, gratuitous, audacious love of God. Forgiveness may be the thing that allows the way forward to be made clear for you.

Perhaps you need to write a letter or make a phone call or visit someone in person and offer them forgiveness. If it's impossible to talk with them—due to death or that you've lost contact or cannot reach out for some other reason—you can go to a place that calms you.

Imagine this person is sitting with you. Tell them what you are sad about, mad about, glad about. Don't be surprised if you are glad for some aspects of the relationship even if you're also glad the relationship has ended. Then offer this person to God. Ask God to forgive this person through you.

I have done this. I went to a park and found a picnic table in an empty area. I spent thirty minutes talking to the person I imagined. I asked God to help me forgive them. I then offered the person forgiveness and sought their forgiveness too. And when I stood up, I felt relief. My body was less tense and I was no longer gripping the past. And it no longer had the same grip on me.

*

When I was researching difficult decision making for this book, I posted on social media that I wanted to interview people who have made difficult decisions. William was one of the people who messaged me.

Several years earlier, William was charged with possession of child pornography and knew instantly it was going to destroy his life.

"After I was convicted, I was released before sentencing so I was still out and about. I was thinking of the future. It was disgraceful and I didn't know if I could live with it. I was very closed off," he told me. He began contemplating whether it was better for his children for him to die or to be in prison.

Many people who face these types of charges consider suicide.

William remembers thinking, "I have screwed up. My family's in a bad situation. Here's one way I can make it better. I was in the military at the time. If I was to die while in active duty, my family would get a lot of money."

As he considered his options, he reflected on his deep desire to love his children well. He realized the only way to try and be a good father to his children was to keep living and rebuild his life.

His crime came from an addiction that was a version of self-medication. "I knew I had to change, but I had no idea how. I didn't understand the problem, much less the solution," he recalled.

In prison, he got involved with Celebrate Recovery, which gave him language for his experiences and ways of coping with difficult feelings. "I had cubby holes to start putting things in. I had a framework to work with. Then things started coming together."

Over time, this group of people loved him back to life. "In Celebrate Recovery, we came up with a thing, *'You spiral down alone. You spiral up in community.'*"

When William said these words, I felt them so deeply. I resonated with how a community of people can ignite our restoration and resurrection.

"The spiritual life is a struggle, a struggle to bring forth new life," explains spiritual director Mary C. Earle.

Through Celebrate Recovery William has gained insight and wants everyone to know, "You're not alone. There are circles out there that do understand. No matter who you are or what you've done, there is a place for you. Things will get better."

William is no longer in prison and continues to meet with one of the men from Celebrate Recovery twice a month. Though he has not seen his children as much as he would like and keeps fighting to be a healthy part of their lives, he is doing all he can to renew his life. When I asked him how things are now, he told me, "I've rebuilt my work life. I started ballroom dancing and made a lot of friends that way. I have work relationships that are going well. I've very intentionally grown my circle of friends. I got a master's degree and managed to purchase a house. There was no before and after. I simply keep looking forward and I expect to be in an even better place."

William was a chaplain in the military, and it was unimaginable he would ever do ministry again given his crime. But even his passion for helping others is being restored, albeit in ways he would not have expected.

"I have taken the lead on doing nursing home ministry. I'm doing volunteer preaching and teaching. I have realized, I'm not Satan or a monster. I can actually be trusted."

Maybe instead of forgiving others, you need to forgive *yourself* for something you did or said or for a whole season of life where you did not live into your own values. Perhaps you need to forgive yourself for a bad decision, or it's finally time to lay down that nagging thought that you could have, should have, shouldn't have. Maybe you made promises that you cannot keep. Maybe you signed a contract that you cannot see through.

You are human. Accept that you make mistakes. You fail and sometimes you morally fail.

You can recover from anything you have said or done. No word or act defines who you are. There is a you there, a dignity, a worth, that is always protected, always preserved.

*

The apostle Paul was walking down a road one day, saw a great light, and fell to the ground. He was blinded for three days until a man named Ananias put his hands on him and gave him a word from God. Something like scales fell from his eyes.

Through these surprising, meaningful experiences, he suddenly realized he needed to stop persecuting Christians and *became one*.

Before this experience, he believed he was being holy by persecuting people who followed Jesus. The very thing he wanted to stop, he joined and expanded. Eventually, he started numerous churches and wrote a considerable amount of the Bible's New Testament.

Likewise, you might be walking one way in your life and believe it is good and right and holy and abruptly realize one day, with God's support, that you need to be doing or thinking something completely different.

Like a snake who has grown out of its skin, you can shed previous versions of yourself. Not only do snakes get new skin so they can expand, they do so to remove harmful parasites.

Sometimes the Spirit of God enters in and shatters your perception of who you are and what you're meant to do with your life.

*

What stories are you telling yourself about who you are?

Think for a moment about some of the major story lines that define you. These usually direct the roles we take on, the way we show up in relationships, the jobs we do, and what we say yes and no to.

I am the steady one.
I am the rock in this family.
I always do the careful thing.
I am the wild one.
I am a mess.
I always know what to say.
I am the achiever.
I am the comforter.

I can fix anything.
I always say yes.
I am the victim.
I am the fighter.

Sometimes particular story lines simply fade over time. They just aren't us anymore.

Sometimes they never were us. Perhaps they seemed noble or we never questioned the person who said, "This is who you are. This is what you should be or should do." We took on these story lines out of obligation or because we thought we had no choice. So, we live out someone else's version of our life story.

As we go through life, sometimes we need to edit story lines from our story so that we can live more fully and with more authenticity.

*

Maybe it is not just your story that needs some editing. Perhaps your story about who God is has been tainted, gotten stale, or become too small. I heard Teresa L. Fry Brown preach once, and she encouraged us to find new names and words for God.

God is, after all,

Alpha and Omega, the Beginning and the End
Jehovah Jireh, the Lord Will Provide
Jehovah Shalom, the Lord Is Peace
Jehovah-Rapha, the Lord Who Heals
Jehovah Tsuri, the Lord Is My Rock
Jehovah Nissi, Mighty Warrior
El Shaddai, God Almighty
El Elyon, God Most High
El Roi, the God Who Sees
Emmanuel, God with Us

There is God, and then there are notions about God. Every once in a while we need to reflect on the conceptions of God that we hold and ask God to help us to see who God really is.

Ask yourself:

- What am I basing my notions of God on?
- When I read stories about Jesus, what does he show me about what God's character is like?
- What new name for God might I call on during this journey?

*

While I was sitting in a coffee shop, two men approached my table, asked to sit with me, and after I told them yes, they asked if I had a word from the Lord for them.

If I had been basically anywhere else in the world, I would have likely kindly declined and felt uncomfortable. Even as a spiritual person, I would have felt odd about strangers asking this question.

But this coffee shop was in Addis Ababa. I was traveling around Ethiopia teaching leadership seminars, and everywhere I went, people would ask the same question.

"Do you have a word from the Lord for me?"

At first the question made me nervous. Over time, I began to anticipate it and, first thing in the morning, would think of something to share. I didn't want to be the only person in Ethiopia who wasn't hearing from God!

I also wanted to seem spiritual and attentive to God's voice. But over time I realized, you weren't meant to always have a response. You were always supposed to be paying attention.

And it worked.

After a few days of fielding this question, I didn't go anywhere without the reminder lingering in the back of my mind that God was speaking if I was willing to listen. I also realized I had the power to ask the question back to others and eventually learned this is how the interaction was intended to work. So, after I responded to the men in the coffee shop, I asked the question back.

I don't remember what I said to them, but to this day, I remember what one of the men said to me.

He did not know it, but I had been in my hotel room for a couple of hours that very morning trying to let go of a relationship. I was having a hard time leaving the past in the past. I had literally been on the floor of my room, listening to inspiring music, and praying for God's help.

"Do you remember when the Israelites were slaves?" he asked with great seriousness.

"Yes!" I replied, mirroring his earnestness.

"And then God freed them and they were in the wilderness? They got frustrated with being in the desert and having to wait for daily food [because they were only given enough for each day] and facing an unknown future."

I imagined the Israelites in my mind's eye, wandering through the wilderness, waiting on God to provide and do something new.

"In their frustration they wanted to go back to how things used to be."

He paused.

"But God did not want them to look back. God wanted them to look to the future."

*

Maybe you need to shed a relationship.

Perhaps you realize that you have tried to create boundaries with someone, tried to make changes, tried to have essential conversations, tried so many things, and the only thing left to do is to detach yourself from this person.

"You can have compassion and empathy for someone and still not want a relationship with them. You can love and care about someone and still not be able to have a relationship with them," explains therapist Amanda E. White. The same goes for workplaces, organizations, groups, and religious communities.

Sometimes we feel so connected to people or things that we struggle to let go even when we know it is time. We can cling to the past in a way that is harmful to our own becoming.

Perhaps you need to shed a pattern like codependency.

One of the most significant revelations I have had about myself over the last few years has been my propensity toward codependency. This is a fancy way of saying I lived many years as a manager of other people.

I felt responsible for others, especially for their problems. I lost sleep over problems no one had asked me to even think about. I had weak boundaries, was overly dependent on others for my sense of self-worth, centered my life around other people, and stayed too long in relationships that didn't work for me—work-wise, romantic, family, and friendships.

My self-written job description was to save people from the consequences of their choices. I was often enmeshed in other people's feelings and actions so much that I had a hard time distinguishing mine from theirs. I took empathy to an unhealthy level.

I was so other-centered that I abandoned myself. The sicker people I loved became, the stronger my reactions.

So, on my own journey toward making difficult decisions, I had to begin to release codependency. I had to do the work. I had to understand its impact on my life, own how I had embodied it for years, and explore all the ways in great detail that it had controlled my life and hurt me and others.

Perhaps codependency is not your thing. Your form of shedding could involve unfastening yourself from expectations others have of you. It's especially difficult to do this when pleasing others is how you have survived. It's not easy to release yourself from the expectations of others when their hopes have been your guiding stars.

You can shed a vision too.

For about twenty years—nearly half of my life now that I'm forty-one—I have had a vision of a table. And until recently, I oriented my life around getting a seat at this table. It was surrounded by capable, intelligent, admired people who have done lots of brilliant things to sit at this table. But it was relatively small.

For years, I strove to be better than others to get a seat. I tried to prove in a calculated, dull, soul-killing way why I belonged at this table, why I was worthy.

Then one day I had an epiphany.

I realized that sitting at this table went against my nature. It would involve shoving myself into a small box, spending time on things I didn't care about, neglecting things I really loved, and worst of all, abandoning some of my deepest held convictions.

Suddenly, I imagined a new kind of table.

At this table, there were tons of open seats and people were enthusiastically waving at me, calling me over to the table, and inviting me to sit down.

"Tell us about yourself," they said. "Tell us what you love. Tell us how we can partner and support each other."

They didn't even know me yet. And they still wanted me at their table. They led with curiosity and assumed my dignity and worth. And best of all, when other people walked by, even people who were like me, more seats appeared.

I shed the old vision and embraced the new one.

I now live on the lookout for tables where people are welcoming others with wild abandon.

Maybe you have had a particular goal for a long time, a picture in your head of where you are going. Maybe you have done everything just right and you're even living that very picture. Maybe you've reached your goal.

Here's the secret about goals: you can reach them only to find out they were not as fulfilling as you hoped they would be.

You know what else? You don't have to reach your goals. And they can change. You can even wake up one day and reframe the way you think of the future and, instead of being goal oriented, you can be motivated by other things like the story you are living toward or the character within that you are trying to develop.

The incredible poet Morgan Harper Nichols describes how hard it can be to let go, but she also notes that it can free something inside "so you can keep traveling / the way you were meant to."

You can delete a chapter. You can edit the paragraph or even the sentence you are in the middle of.

You can let it end.

You can take a departure.

You can let it break.

You can narrate the story differently.

You can make room for something new.

FIELD NOTES TO SELF

- Subtraction is holy.
- Practice forgiveness even when it's undeserved.
- If you're stuck, you can edit your story line.

SIFTING

When You Have Contending Convictions

May God give you the grace never to sell yourself short;
Grace to risk something big for something good; and
Grace to remember the world is now too dangerous for anything but the
truth and too small for anything but love.

—Rev. William Sloane Coffin,
The Collected Sermons of William Sloane Coffin

Anne Hutchinson had a dynamic personality and an ability to articulate ideas in a compelling way. She had a deep affection and admira-
tion for her father and grew up to be a lot like him, independent with
a high sense of principle.

"Had she been born into a later age, Mrs. Hutchinson might have
crusaded for women's rights, or even wielded a hatchet for temper-
ance's sake. But, for better or worse, her lot was cast in the seventeenth
century, and her hand was to be felt in a theological tempest which
shook the infant colony of Massachusetts to its very foundations,"
writes historian Emery John Battis.

After her father died, she married William Hutchinson, who adored her and was willing to follow her anywhere. Anne gave birth to fifteen children between 1613 and 1636.

She started traveling to Boston several times a year with her husband, and while he worked, she listened to John Cotton preach. Cotton talked about the grace of God, and Anne was captivated. As she reflected more and more on the idea of grace, she concluded that it's all grace and not the work of humans that leads to God's presence in people. Anne determined that if someone felt God's presence in their heart, that was enough.

In 1630, two of her children died a month apart. One was fourteen, and the other was eight. Anne struggled for meaning in the senselessness of the universe after their deaths. She spent a lot of time in prayer and solitude. One day, she was given a revelation from God that it was imperative that all ministers teach about the grace of God.

After this revelation, she started commenting on sermons at weekly gatherings in her home, helping other women to understand more deeply what they were hearing. Not long after, women were gathering from all over town at her home to listen to her. Then Anne began preaching and sharing her own views, explaining the ways pastors were focusing on what people could do to earn God's salvation versus God's grace. Eventually, these gatherings became so popular that the women's husbands started joining them. For a time, Anne was supported in her ministry by the pastors of her congregation. But then in 1636, they began to wonder whether she was passing on unorthodox views.

Eventually Anne was tried for heresy. She was called a heretic and an instrument of the devil, and was condemned to banishment by the court. Anne was then exiled and excommunicated because of her beliefs.

Today, there is a statue in Boston that honors her as a champion for religious freedom and integral to the history of women in ministry.

Question: How do I know what is true?
Prayer: Teach me.

As a professor, I occasionally encountered students who showed up in class with clenched fists, ready to fight new perspectives. They were pursuing higher education seemingly not to gain new insight but rather to reaffirm what they already knew.

They sat back in their chairs, arms folded. Sometimes they slouched with their heads buried in their laptops. Often, they would pretend to take notes, but their posture and lack of participation in the class conversation indicated their heads were somewhere else.

The students who came with open hands inspired me as a teacher.

They had strong convictions and cared deeply about God, the world, others, and virtues like love. They had stories to share, and they were ready to explain why they felt the way they did. At the same time, they met new ideas—from books, from peers, from me—with curiosity.

We can both hold and receive with open hands.

If your fists are clenched during this journey, nothing can be given to you and it will be difficult for you to leave anything behind. But we can hold, receive, and set down beliefs when we travel with open hands.

Hold your beliefs lightly. Let them change when they need to.

The idea of shifting beliefs can be scary. But remember: you probably once thought a McDonald's Happy Meal was the best dinner in the world or that putting on a jacket was so terrible it was worth a tantrum. This journey needs room for new views to be revealed to you and for old beliefs to be excavated and then revised, refined, expanded, or discarded as necessary.

*

As I interviewed Gen on the phone for this book, her passion for helping other people to be freed from horrendous situations like hers was evident.

The abuse she endured lasted more than twenty years. For most of that time, Gen believed the Christian response to the abuse was to pray, stay, submit, try harder, forgive, forget. Gen and her children were isolated from family and had very few friends.

"We had no one who we could be honest with; it was hidden. With domestic violence, you can't live your truth. It was his words against my kids' words if he killed me," she reflected.

As she told me her story, Gen said that eventually daily death threats caused her to realize she had to do something different.

Thankfully, a spiritual awakening had slowly been dawning within her.

A couple of years prior, she received a brochure in the mail from the family crisis shelter in her town that said, "Love shouldn't hurt," and it outlined abusive behaviors. It was the first time Gen had language for what she experienced. She wrote down some of the things the brochure said and threw the brochure away so her husband wouldn't find it. She put the paper with notes in a hidden spot in their home.

Gen then decided to do some Web searching using the words from the brochure on various nights while her husband was away at work. She continued to take notes for herself from the Web searching in another hidden document.

Her Internet searches led to a sermon series from a pastor in Oregon on abuse. "He talked about how abuse is against God's design for the family. This pastor specifically said, 'God does not require that you stay in an abusive marriage. God will not hold you in bondage to an abusive marriage.'"

It was the first time she had ever heard a pastor talk about abuse in the home and speak out against it.

Suddenly, her old belief of "stay, submit, try harder" was being challenged by a new belief, "God does not require that you stay in an abusive marriage."

Months later, Gen's family ended up in a new church. It was not speaking out against abuse like the pastor she heard online. But one Sunday God reached out to her through a woman she met there.

Gen and another mom started talking about their lives while trying to soothe their active toddlers in the church's "cry room." Gen found herself identifying with the woman's story of domestic violence. She gave Gen "language" for what she was going through, and she "was identifying with someone who had similar experiences."

The other mom had even found the *same sermon series* Gen had listened to, and they bonded over it. "Neither one of us had ever heard anything like that. Changing my beliefs about stay, pray, submit meant someone preaching to me from a different mindset," she explained.

Whoever that Oregon pastor is, thank you. Thank you. Thank you.

Gen's husband threatened to kill her if she ever got the authorities involved. That was the line in the sand, to never call for help. And she had not contacted any kind of help for twenty years.

But one day—two years after she received that brochure from the family crisis shelter—Gen dialed 911. She was distressed because her husband was about to attack someone else, so she did what previously had been unthinkable.

All the information gathering over time, those significant moments where God guided her through others, the same kind of message in different forms—the brochure, the online Oregon preacher, the woman in the cry room—had created a shift in her perspective and created within her new capacity to take action.

The police didn't file a report, but one of them said something that Gen took as the voice of God. "If you fear what he will do to you when he gets home from work, then clear out while he is gone."

After twenty years of abuse, fear, and numerous death threats, Gen left with her kids and went into hiding.

The first year was all about safety, so they had to be vigilant. At the same time, she knew they needed to develop relationships and make a life beyond the abuse they had endured.

One of the most surprising gifts was getting involved at a local community theater. The people who were a part of this organization became a family for them that Gen called "hugely healing." The people they met in that community helped her and her kids see that there are people in this world who aren't abusive.

After the first year, Gen realized she could finally go back to school. Her ex-husband made her drop out of college, but he no longer had control over her life. For Gen, realizing that she had agency and autonomy and could continue her education was big. It was another significant leap toward a different kind of life for herself.

Her old beliefs were being replaced by new ones.

Other people could be trustworthy. She was capable of getting a degree like she had always hoped. Eventually, Gen joined the board of directors for the family crisis shelter that had helped her when she escaped years earlier.

Gen finished her degree. She is a survivor who teaches churches how to better care for the people in their communities who experience violence in their homes. She leads trainings and gives tools that equip faith leaders to provide valuable support for other survivors. Her trainings teach pastors how to talk about and preach against abuse and hold people who abuse accountable as well as how to partner with their local family crisis shelter.

She told me what the shifts in her life have meant to her, saying, "It was gratifying and gave me purpose. God was saving me from ultimate destruction to change the landscape and help pastors and churches understand domestic violence and improve pastoral care for survivors."

*

An internal conflict, crisis, or crucible experience usually creates cognitive dissonance. Like Gen, you realize suddenly that a long-held belief is being challenged by a new viewpoint, insight, or principle. You try to make sense of everything you are thinking, and it's a struggle. Your mind has a kind of war going on within it.

Cognitive dissonance can feel disorienting, overwhelming, and terrifying. It can also be a gateway to truth, freedom, and eventually joy.

When I read the stories of people and interviewed people who made bold, difficult choices, I realized many of them were compelled by new ideas that impacted their beliefs and values that then demanded an adjustment to their perspective, their habits, or overall life.

Figuring out what decision to make often requires wrestling with what beliefs are being challenged. Do you have beliefs that appear to be in conflict with one another?

We have three primary ways to resolve cognitive dissonance.

The first way is rejection.

You decide two things can't both be true, so you reject one of them. I call this "release and catch"—you release one belief and catch another.

This option involves some kind of loss. Sometimes this loss feels like relief. Sometimes you feel wildly grateful that you can let go of a belief because it stifled you, created pain, wasn't of God.

Other times, the loss is painful and disorienting. We can lose a sense of trust in ourselves, others, or institutions we care about. We can lose our sense of connection or respect. We can lose our confidence. We can lose a relationship, our religion, or our sense of who we are.

When you lose something substantial—your identity, your religious community, your job—you need a purposeful plan for healing (there is guidance for how to create this kind of plan in chapter 10). It is possible to rebuild your life. In some cases, this is precisely what you need even if it breaks your heart and creates a difficult path.

Either way, rejecting a previously held conviction that was significant to you requires a very intentional healing process, like Gen's, that involves the support and care of others, therapy and spiritual direction and counsel, deep commitment to self-compassion, and soaking up God's love through restorative habits and rituals.

*

The second way to resolve cognitive dissonance is expansion.

This is a lightbulb kind of moment where you don't so much replace one belief with another but your views are sharpened, deepened, or enhanced in some way.

Jesse was also willing to be interviewed about his marriage. It is a very different situation from Gen's story, but it also involved wrestling with various beliefs. Jesse and his wife, Celine, first explored separating in 2019. For several years, they lived like roommates with no sexual encounters and no intimate conversation. They shared physical space but largely lived unconnected lives, even visiting their families separately.

"There was so much shame," Jesse reflected during our conversation. There was shame about what people might think if they knew about the state of their marriage, shame about bodies, desires, sex, sexuality, and intimacy.

He realizes now that his fundamentalist Christian upbringing created no space for understanding any of these things. So instead, he experienced repression and dysfunction, a kind of imprisonment in his own skin.

Through counsel, Jesse has realized his fear, insecurity, and hang-ups about bodies and sex damaged his relationship with Celine. He brought this baggage into his marriage. His wife was his first sexual experience, and he had no resources for navigating this intimate relationship in healthy ways.

Rather than see these things initially, though, he asked other kinds of questions. Would I be happier with someone else? Would she? Are we a good match for one another? He explained during our conversation that they had significant differences in their spirituality when they married and still did, differences that caused him to question their compatibility after they were married, especially since his vocation shifted from wanting to be a part of the film industry to wanting to be a chaplain and a priest. This switch also surprised his wife. His newfound calling only deepened their sense of disconnection.

Eventually, Jesse felt the weight of a massive decision.

Should he get divorced or stay married?

He viewed his decision as a long conversation that happened with God over time, a conversation that involved reading Scripture, multiple sessions with his spiritual director, counsel from trusted friends and family members, experiences with colleagues on the chaplain team, and deep discussions with his wife. Each in its own way helped him to stretch his imagination for what was possible as well as his perspective on his life.

Jesse's spiritual director created space for him to address his fear and anxiety around the whole realm of sex. He said it was incredibly freeing to talk openly with another person with similar faith commitments who was completely comfortable with her body and desires. Through direct and helpful dialogue about once-ignored or whispered topics, he realized that sexuality is more beautiful, complex, mysterious, and wonderful than he ever knew it to be.

Owning his goodness was another huge step in Jesse's liberation from toxic thinking. Over time Jesse could hear God saying, "I am in your corner. I love you."

And eventually, he also learned to say these words to himself. He realized that his words have power and the way he feels about himself matters deeply.

Embracing his identity of an interfaith hospital chaplain has allowed him to both hold his convictions as a Christian and learn from people who have different but often helpful insights from their traditions. His vision for ministry went from the macro to the micro. He thought, "I can also apply these lessons to my marriage and relationship with Celine's family. I don't have to judge them or have these expectations or an agenda for their life."

He also has two clergy friends he has regular conversation with, and they often say to one another, "This is a shame-free zone. We are not going to shame each other or ourselves." He has done a lot of learning and unlearning around stereotypes of men and roles in marriage too. For example, he has embraced that he is a sensitive person and now even sees this as a good thing.

Over time, the freedom and shame-free talks he experienced with his spiritual director and clergy friends and even himself translated to the conversations he had with Celine. He became practiced at being more open, vulnerable, honest, and unrestricted, which nurtured intimacy in his marriage.

Previously Celine couldn't risk opening up to him about her dreams or her passions, because he was withholding from her and wasn't giving her his full self.

Suddenly, Celine "really put herself out there and took some risks. Early on in the relationship, I really pursued her. When we were at the crossroads, really trying to figure out what to do, she really pursued me. She said things like, 'I choose this and I choose you even though it's hard. I still want you and want to fight for this and our life together.'" He found this attractive and compelling.

He began to ask new questions: Who would stick with me through thick and thin like her? Who would walk with me at my worst like she has? What if we do the work to become the perfect person for one another? He found himself saying, "I really want to be on this journey with Celine."

During our conversation he also said, "Could I have a different type of relationship with a different woman? Of course. But this is the person I chose and have done life with for twelve years. It would be very traumatic to go through a divorce and dividing our lives and separating our friends. I weighed the cost."

A quote that has stayed with Jesse is, "Fantasy is what people want, but reality is what they need. And I just retired from the fantasy part." He first heard this on Lauryn Hill's MTV Unplugged album. "Now I am wanting to live in reality with my people and my person," he said confidently.

Through Jesse's various forms of cognitive dissonance, his perspective on his marriage was expanded, refined, and sharpened, and he came to see Celine as a trusted friend and partner.

When I asked him how things are going since they decided to stay married, he said, "We are creating the relationship we want to have, together, in conversation. We are breaking new ground. It was a surprise to both of us that we have this second chance."

*

The third way to resolve cognitive dissonance is to embrace paradox. This happens when you believe two seemingly conflicting things are true.

You are capable and you are clumsy. You need boundaries and freedom, rules and play. You are unique and imitative. Lives are limitless and finite. Work is essential and work is unreliable. Communities of worship are supportive and fragmented. People are randomly kind and deliberately cold-blooded. Mentors can help us and mentors disappoint us. Children are heart-expanders and heartbreakers. Romantic relationships are born from desire and woundedness. Friendship helps me recognize that I can be deeply known and never truly known. Education is constructive and disruptive. Dreams are invigorating and crushing. Silence is peaceful and scary. Darkness is clarifying and terrifying. Light is revealing and overwhelming. The world is spectacular and ruthless.

Welcome to the world of *and*, to the world of paradox.

When I interviewed Roseline about her work journey, a third option for dealing with contending convictions became apparent. Roseline was working on a grant at an institution. The people at the organization she worked for loved her work, and her boss wanted her to stay. But Roseline couldn't imagine working at the institution after the grant ended because she was already considering leaving her role before the grant work was complete.

She hated sitting all day at a computer, and while she felt fulfilled by certain parts of her job, the corporate structure related to her work wasn't jiving with her and at times felt quite stifling. She had been feeling she should move on to something more creative.

Roseline described coming from a low-income, immigrant family background and explained that in her family, "You don't leave good-paying jobs." Even though she had savings to lean on, she found herself asking, "Who quits their job? Who would be silly enough to do that?"

For a while, Roseline felt a push-pull within her as to what she should do and when and how everything would come together—her passions, gifts, calling, finances.

Only adding to her confusion was remembering when her job was an answer to prayer. This job that she was struggling to do used to be the thing that she wanted. It distressed her that the thing she had prayed for was now the thing she was feeling she needed to let go of and move on from.

But she couldn't ignore what was happening. One day she realized she was having physical symptoms in her body due to her work environment. Roseline's muscles began seizing up and her back was hurting. She was getting regular headaches. And on an especially difficult day, before walking into work, she felt like she couldn't breathe in the parking lot.

Reflecting, she said, "My vision about my possibilities was myopic so I wasn't seeing what was around me, the other options."

One of the books a friend recommended to her was *Necessary Endings*, which explores knowing when to quit and say, "I've had enough." It contains a story about a man having to mentally psych himself up in the parking lot to walk into work.

Obviously, this stood out to Roseline. Synchronicity.

Roseline also read another book about the ways in which our bodies know about decisions before our minds do, and this caused her to listen to her body's inner cues.

Over time, she noticed the way her body was reacting at work versus in other spaces. Her pain became chronic, and she was trying to find a way to make it stop. One Sunday night she noticed that her muscles were tensing up again and suddenly made the connection that it was because she needed to go back to work on Monday morning. She realized that when she was away from work, her pain went away.

She thought about her life and her various jobs. A previous role came into her mind that was similar to the job with the grant. She realized she had despised sitting in one place at that job too, and this caused her to reflect on her likes and dislikes in general.

"This was a slow revealing for me over a number of months," she said. She started to realize what truly enlivened her, and eventually she realized she did in fact have options.

Roseline's mother passed away, but she still hears her voice in her head. They had a close, loving relationship, and Roseline still receives guidance from her mom through their shared experiences that echo in her heart. "My mom used to say, the expression in Creole, is 'God's grace hovers,'" Roseline recalled.

Roseline explained that this means when you are in God's will, God will give you the strength to do whatever you need to be doing. She said, "That's how you know you're in God's flow." On the other hand, "When you're going uphill and losing your strength, you need to find the cloud of God's grace." It is God's grace hovering that gives you that extra jolt and allows you to be able to navigate a challenging ordeal."

Roseline's mom was making connections between our lives and what Moses and the Israelites experienced. God led them as a pillar of fire by night and a pillar of cloud by day. Her mom had always encouraged her to consider, "Is the cloud of God's grace still on that or has it moved on? If not, you need to find where it has moved on to and catch up."

As her mother's words and questions lingered in her soul, she suddenly realized she had been called to the job she had on the grant *and* needed to leave her job when the cloud of God's grace moved on.

Along the way, Roseline did what she called "unlearning and mind shifts," especially regarding her perception of herself and her own success. In fact, she is still making internal changes. This decision process meant changing not just the nature of her work but also how she views her gifts, her identity, and her vocation.

After leaving her job on the grant, Roseline's aches went away and her body started to recalibrate.

And after coming out of the meeting where she gave notice of her resignation to her boss, she got her first major art commission for the whole month's salary that she thought she would be missing and would need savings to cover.

"It felt like God taking care of me. This was confirmation for me. I didn't have the full picture but this was a lamp to my feet."

Perhaps the cognitive dissonance you have experienced requires you to enjoy the word "and." In an enlightening conversation with my best friend of umpteen years, Molly Galbraith, she talked about the massive difference between two simple words: "but" and "and."

The word "but" closes down the mind and often gives us the perception that we need to choose. For example, "I want to start my own business but I'm a new mom." On the other hand, the word "and" opens up possibilities and invites the brain to churn and problem-solve.

As with the case of paradox, two seemingly conflicting thoughts can be true at the same time with an "and": I want to start my own business *and* I'm a new mom.

There are many beliefs you may hold during this journey that may seem like opposites but could be embraced as equally true:

You are resilient and you need a break.
You don't like the way things are and you need to stay.
You love this person and you need to leave them.
You were sure and things changed.
You are kind and you have boundaries.
You are having a hard time and you want to keep trying.
You felt called to the work you are doing and you feel called to something new.
You love where you live and you feel drawn to living somewhere else.
You don't like the way the relationship is and you still want the relationship.
You are heartbroken and you are thankful.
You forgave them and you can't be in a relationship with them.

Much of the spiritual life involves honoring paradox.

FIELD NOTES TO SELF

- You can release an idea you no longer believe.
- Don't be afraid to expand an existing belief.
- Embrace paradox.

SELECTING

When You Are Choosing between Different Values

I carried an ache under my ribs that was like radar: it told me I was miles away from the world I intended to make for my son and myself.

—Joy Harjo, *Crazy Brave*

Amma Syncletica was a desert mother who lived in the fourth century. Desert mothers were wise guides who cared for people's souls. They lived secluded lifestyles out of restlessness and a desire to have the highest values animate their lives.

During this period of history, churches became more and more aligned with governments and their priorities, and over time it became hard to distinguish religious values from a ruler's values.

Fascinating how history repeats itself again and again.

Amma was reportedly wealthy and beautiful, and people expected her to marry and flourish in city life. After her parents died, though, Amma gave her entire inheritance to the poor.

Amma and her sister decided they were called to a life of simplicity, generosity, hospitality, and mercy, values that couldn't be lived by living out other people's expectations or nurturing the values of a nation-state. They made the difficult decision to leave their home and live in a crypt.

Yes, you read that correctly.

In order to live out their religious commitments, they had to leave behind what they were socialized to be and do, and seek the life they felt they were meant to live. For them, life in the crypt was unknown territory, literally and figuratively.

Beyond this, the symbolism of death that a crypt holds demonstrates what it took for them to live for the values they felt called to live for. It took death of one way of life, and their choice meant a largely secluded life.

Living by worthy values doesn't always mean living a more pleasurable, fun life. Sometimes pursuing a life worthy of all that we are means opening ourselves to more hardship, loss, and insecurity.

You may wonder why Amma and her sister could possibly prefer a crypt to the city, poverty instead of wealth, isolation over community. Why would they choose a more difficult life?

For them, to live in the city was to live imprisoned to someone else's agenda and desires. To live in the city was to deny the truths they had come to know. It would mean abandoning themselves and ignoring God's invitations to something deeper and bigger.

Perhaps this is why Jesus said, "What good will it be for someone to gain the whole world, yet forfeit their soul? Or what can anyone give in exchange for their soul?"

Amma's new way of living cost her nearly everything she had previously known and owned. Amma would say that she lived free, though, because she didn't live with the fear of loss and because desire was unable to consume her.

After a long time of solitude, other women who were looking for guidance came to Amma. She sensed that God wanted her to share all she had learned. She began mentoring women who were trying to discern their vocations.

She lived into her eighties, and her sayings are recorded in a book dedicated to the words of the desert fathers. Amma is now known as a saint of the Christian tradition.

Question: What is mine to do?
Prayer: Enlighten me.

For years I kept my nose to the grindstone. I had a full-time job and then side gigs that eventually equaled another full-time job. I was the queen of hustle and grind. My refrain was, "I'm busy and exhausted."

My tendency was to blame myself rather than the systems that fostered overwork and burnout. I labeled myself a workaholic who had trouble saying no. My other inclination was to do more. I imagined if I could just have a more thorough morning routine, for example, I'd feel better. But no matter what I did, I only grew more emotionally and mentally exhausted.

During one fall semester, I knew something had to change because of my consistent desire to escape my everyday life. I had experienced chronic stress for a decade. The political work environment was also killing my spirit.

I was about to go up for tenure as a professor. Tenure is one of the most significant promotions a professor can receive, and I was all but guaranteed I would get it. Yet as I imagined it coming, I kept wondering whether it was for me.

If I came to life in my twenties, I died a hundred deaths in my thirties. These deaths came in several forms.

One was the loss of a veil I had worn over my eyes all of my life. An innocent trust and belief that if I can just get to the right institution, be the right kind of woman, make a difference in the lives of my students and parishioners in my care, the sexism will stop.

I endured sexism throughout my career at basically every institution I worked at—churches and in higher education—and I had always believed I could help turn things around.

Over the last twenty years, sexism happened in one-on-one conversations where I experienced jokes about my gender and my appearance and the fact that "You don't look like a pastor!" And not just by men; very often this was one of the favorite jokes of women. I always wanted to ask, "What does a pastor look like?"

I have heard many offhand remarks about my clothing, assessments I have not witnessed others making about the men around me. For example, I spoke at a retreat. I was the only woman on the speaking team. I intentionally wore black attire all weekend so I wouldn't draw attention to myself with my clothing. (It is exhausting how much female leaders have to think about what they wear.) On the third day of the retreat a man said, "I noticed you wore black all weekend. What's the deal with that? Why no color?" I asked the men who spoke if anyone mentioned what they wore, and of course, no one did.

I was told in several one-on-one discussions what I shouldn't be doing because I am a female. There was a particularly painful conversation with a professor during my PhD studies where I was compared with disgust to "women like me."

There were group settings where I was labeled "quite opiniated for a woman," and work meetings where bullying and intimidation tactics were used to try and put me in "my place." During one annual review, after formally being given the highest marks possible on my work performance (which was required given the standards I had met), paperwork was pushed aside and I was privately warned to be cautious and threatened with "I would hate for things to get hard for you around here."

One of my former bosses lost his ministerial license because of sexual harassment.

And I have been in classrooms where students have questioned my abilities and authority through evaluations, replies in assignments, and statements in front of their peers. I'm not talking about the thoughtful, constructive feedback I have received. I am writing here about straightforward actions and words that were made at Christian institutions because a student thought a woman shouldn't be teaching them or because a student thought they could disrespect a woman because they saw her as less important or worthy of respect than male colleagues.

I know that these things were not imagined because my therapist said, "That was a threat. You know that, right?" And because colleagues and peers of those students and congregants have pulled me to the side on too many occasions and whispered about what happened and checked on me. I was asked constantly, "How do you do it? How do you deal with this? How have you gotten to where you are?"

And I responded with some version of "This is how it is," or "Female voices matter," or, of course, my favorite, "I am busy and exhausted."

The most ironic way I know about the sexism of churches and Christian institutions is the celebration.

Usually, the very fact that I was hired, on the team, noted, speaking, included, was extraordinary. A woman is here! Can you believe it? I used to think it was special that I was the only woman in a room of men. I sort of wore it as a badge of honor. It should have infuriated me.

The pain of my thirties also came with the literal deaths of multiple people I loved and in traumatic ways. I write about the pain of some of these deaths extensively in another book, *The Gravity of Joy*.

As I wrote before, I woke up one morning and realized I had a significant decision to make.

One day I had to choose what mattered more.

I could choose dedication to the cause of lifting women up in the spaces where there were already not enough women, a promotion, and a job title people understand. I could choose to seek more improvement, more equity, achievements, and ladder climbing. I could have even more reputable goals.

Or I could choose my mental, physical, spiritual, relational, and emotional health by literally having space for therapy, for being outside, for time with God and people I love, for recovery, for healing. My integrity was also on the line, so I could have more harmony between my convictions, actions, and principles and my sources of income.

In other words, I could live more truthfully and participate in my holistic healing, *or* I could keep advancing and advocating for women, have a very reliable income, get lots of money for retirement, and get more respect and more accolades. At that time, in those circumstances, I could not have it all. I had to choose.

We often think difficult decisions are about things like time, money, regret, and failure. But behind each of these is at least one deeply held value. Time is about who or what you value that gets your time. A value for money points to a deeper value for something like taking care of people we love or living freely or having stability.

Truly, the thing that makes important decisions wildly difficult is choosing between values. And often we initially feel like we are picking between values that feel equally important or good to us. This doesn't necessarily need to be the case for the rest of your life, but for a season, this is what needs to happen.

When I surveyed the lives of people who made difficult decisions, one thing that kept coming up was that they *couldn't not do* what they did.

*

Centuries after Amma and her sister, John and Vera Mae Perkins also sacrificed a comfortable, prospering life. Though they had a meaningful, thriving ministry in California, John felt called to go back to his native Mississippi. He sensed that God was inviting him to help his people.

When he first shared his new vision with Vera Mae, she resisted. She knew about the poverty and racial injustice in Mississippi; she had been born and raised there too. She wanted to protect their family.

They found themselves with two very different visions for their shared life guided by two sets of values.

Over time, John became weaker physically. He lost weight and was diagnosed with ulcers. His body was speaking to them both. One day he couldn't get out of bed.

Vera Mae found herself praying to let go of her own will and giving her situation to God. She even felt like she should tell John that she was willing to go back to Mississippi with him.

Within days, John's strength returned. As he prepared to move their family, he recovered.

The Perkins family felt called to minister in Mississippi despite the lack of opportunities for education for their children and despite the conditions of where they would live, including the fact that they were moving to a racially divided place at the beginning of the civil rights movement that would put their entire family in danger.

It is even wilder that John would be willing to go back to where he had grown up given what he experienced. When John was just sixteen years young, his older brother, Clyde, was shot and killed by a law officer. Having just returned from war with a Purple Heart, Clyde came home to be killed in his own community while waiting in a line designated for Black people at a movie theater.

To many outsiders, the Perkinses likely appeared irrational and unwise. The thing is, what can look wise to others may be foolish for you, and what may look foolish to others may be incredibly wise for you.

Instead of clinging to the American dream and all they had done to better their lives, they moved their family to nurture their higher values.

Stephen E. Berk writes in his biography of John, "As John thought about the alternative values of God's kingdom, as opposed to the values of the world, he began to realize that when he joined himself to God he took on 'a whole new structure of life.' That's the way he put it years later."

The Perkins family gave up a sense of security, stability, and safety as well as advancement and opportunity for inner peace, genuine belonging, and a deeper sense of meaning and purpose.

*

I invite you to do some digging. When you think about your decision, what values are at stake?

Consider making a list right now. If you have never done a values inventory, there is a helpful tool in the appendix to assist you.

Some of the most compelling values for complex decisions that we live for are integrity, authenticity, legacy, purpose, love, justice, freedom, security, well-being, wholeness, goodness, dedication, loyalty, duty, and belonging.

I invite you to reflect on your list of values and consider which values you cannot help but to live. There are a few ways to assess values that will help you to determine which ones are worth living toward during this stage of your life. In fact, embedded in this sentence is one way of assessing your values: worthiness.

What value or set of values is worthier?

In other words, which value or set of values encourages a kind of life that is *good* for you, for your family, for your community, for the world? The good here could be thought of in terms of peace, wholeness, truth, meaning.

Similarly, think about where each value or set of values leads you. If you are motivated by one set, what kind of life would you be making? And if you are motivated by the other, what kind of life would you be nurturing?

Attend to your body. What happens in your body when you consider each value or set of values? If you feel resistance when you meditate on a certain noble value, investigate it. If you feel a magnetic pull when you meditate on a certain noble value, explore it. What truths are revealed by the resistance or the magnetic pull? What can you learn?

Sometimes we have values because we are trying to imitate or honor people we respect.

"I must listen to my life telling me who I am. I must listen for the truths and values at the heart of my own identity, not the standards by which I must live—but the standards by which I cannot help but live if I am living my life," writes Parker Palmer. Values can be admirable and still *not* be values that we should live for.

Ask God for help. Listen to your life, your heart.

What values are truly yours to embody?

*

For the Perkinses, social change and inner change went hand in hand.

They did ministry through community development and took care of people spiritually and physically in an integrated way. Over time, they created a day-care center, youth program, church, cooperative farm, thrift store, housing repair ministry, health center, and adult education program.

They were also heavily invested in the civil rights movement, which meant their children were among the first Black children to attend an all-white school in Mississippi.

The very safety they knew was at stake when moving was disrupted when John was brutally beaten by officers and put in prison after attempting to free Black college students from Tougaloo College and Jackson State University who had been jailed for freedom-marching with the Perkinses.

Despite hardships and having only gotten the opportunity to finish third grade, John has seventeen honorary doctorates and his community-development work in both Mississippi and California continues to impact people's lives in significant ways. The work of the Perkinses has become a model and inspiration for how to cultivate significant and lasting change.

We look back on history and we think, how did that person do what they did? Why are they remembered? How did they do such beautiful things?

Most couldn't *not* do it.

They decided what was worthier. They embraced the surrendering, loss, and grief that often come with selecting values and pursuing a life worth living.

FIELD NOTES TO SELF

- Decide which values are most important during this season.
- Live values that are worthy of everything you are.
- The right choice doesn't always feel good.

SEARCHING

When You Are Experiencing Analysis Paralysis

The glory of God is a human being fully alive.

—Irenaeus, *Against Heresies*

As an extraordinary competitor and the first Black athlete to play Major League Baseball (MLB) in the modern era, Jackie Robinson is one of the most iconic baseball players of all time. But joining the Brooklyn Dodgers in 1947 was a difficult decision for him and his wife.

At that moment in sports history, the MLB was reserved for white players while Black players were consigned to the underfunded and poorly managed Negro League. But Branch Rickey, general manager of the Dodgers, wanted to change that. Rickey carried with him the memory of a Black athlete he'd seen abused decades earlier during his own time as a player. And when he had the chance to do something about how players of color were treated, Rickey stepped up.

But Rickey knew signing a Black ballplayer to the Dodgers was the easy part. The player himself would bear the brunt of the public's racist disapproval. So, he needed a player who would willingly allow name-calling and rejection from fans, sportswriters, other teams, coaches, and even his own teammates. Basically, anyone and everyone.

In his autobiography, Jackie Robinson writes about the kind of ballplayer Branch Rickey was looking for: "He had to be able to stand up in the face of merciless persecution and not retaliate. . . . His ability to turn the other cheek had to be predicated on his determination to gain acceptance. Once having proven his ability as a player, teammate, and man, he had to be able to cast off humbleness, and stand up as a full-fledged participant, whose triumph did not carry the poison of bitterness."

So not only did Jackie Robinson need to be an incredible baseball player, he needed to be willing to be persecuted without becoming bitter. What an order! "Plenty of times I wanted to haul off when somebody insulted me for the color of my skin, but I had to hold to myself. I knew I was kind of an experiment. The whole thing was bigger than me," explains Robinson.

Jackie agreed to Branch Rickey's "noble experiment," as it has been called, because he was willing to lose personally for the greater gain for humanity, and not just during his baseball career, but for the rest of his life.

Jackie credits his wife, Rachel (Rae), for comforting him and helping him to remain steadfast on the days he needed it most. "Rachel's understanding love was a powerful antidote for the poison of being taunted by fans, sneered at by fellow-players, and constantly mistreated because of my blackness," he writes.

Even off the field, he persevered through mistreatment, harassment, and racism. When he was on buses and told to go to the back, he did. He says, "I remembered the things Rae and I had said to each other during the months we had tried to prepare ourselves for exactly this kind of ordeal. We had agreed that I had no right to lose my temper and jeopardize the chances of all the [B]lacks who would follow me if I could help break down the barriers. So we moved back to the very last seat, as indicated by the driver."

Sometimes, like Jackie Robinson, we make decisions that prioritize long-term goals over extreme personal cost and even injustice.

He chose the struggle because joining the Dodgers wasn't just about his own career, it was about all the future careers he could make possible. His decision to join the Dodgers was just one of many difficult decisions he made that were centered on creating a more equitable society.

> *Question: What am I being led to do?*
> *Prayer: Show me.*

We are mostly only familiar with reward and punishment. We imagine: If I can just work hard enough at getting this right, I will get the life I earned. And we end up asking questions like: How can I be the kind of person God blesses? How can I make a decision that avoids pain, grief, regret, being uncomfortable? Decision making gets relegated to blessings and vengeance, pleasure and pain, pros and cons.

But of course, sometimes people who do good get punished and sometimes evildoers get rewarded. But more than that, this theoretical system of rewards and punishments ignores the true character of God. While I much prefer other people getting what they deserve, "God gives his best—the sun to warm and the rain to nourish—to everyone, regardless: the good and bad, the nice and nasty." Personally, I'd like God to just be good to me no matter what I do and treat others the way they deserve to be treated. Alas, God doesn't work like that. God is merciful to all.

The reward and punishment mind-set can also encourage us to ask unhelpful questions and sometimes pursue unworthy aims.

Rather than being focused on specific outcomes related to a specific decision, what might it look like to be focused on the bigger picture of what our lives are looking toward and the kind of people we are trying to become? To do this we can ask questions informed by the larger scope of our lives, and the kind of character we are trying to develop.

Try a set of questions that focuses on a key value.
Something like:

- What choice produces good fruit (e.g., love, joy, peace, patience, kindness, goodness, faithfulness, gentleness, or self-control)? For someone else, the community, me?
- What pathway leads to integrity, to simplicity, to forgiveness, to justice, to accountability, to responsibility, to belonging (to pertinent values and virtues related to the situation)?
- What decision contributes to wholeness and helps those who are impacted to live an undivided life?
- What decision contributes to holistic well-being (spiritual, physical, mental, emotional, relational)?
- How might this decision contribute to the development of truthfulness and healing?

We can't ask every one of these questions about each decision we make. We can't keep all the possible good values in mind. The inner work from chapter 8 on selecting, ranking, and choosing values for this season of your life is important work that will help you to be clearer about how your decision might contribute to meaningful aims and thus what questions to ask.

As we are searching for what path to choose, there are also fixations that can cause a psychological roadblock during our decision-making process that we need to break down.

The first is enoughness. As in, if I just keep going in this way or change my life in that way, I will eventually get to enough. I will have enough power, enough time, enough stuff, enough accolades.

The same can be said of the thought of more. If we keep going in the same direction, we could have more—more happiness, more money, more freedom.

Or maybe you are more drawn to the idea of better. If I keep waiting, things will get better. This person will change. The circumstances will improve. If I just keep waiting, what I need will eventually come.

If enoughness, more, or better are creating mental roadblocks for you, spend some time defining them. What does enough or more or better actually mean for your life and the people who will be impacted by your decision? What does it take to get to enough, more, or better?

When I started working for myself, I was trying to figure out how to not run myself into the ground working all of the time. One of my mental roadblocks was enoughness. Once I worked on a budget and had a concrete goal in my mind of how much money was enough to make each month, I was able to stop taking on more work than I needed to.

You may also feel stuck because of a longing for certainty that may never come or a desire to cling to security that is likely not as sturdy as you imagine. Sure, some degree of security or certainty is helpful. But in this life, beyond the love of God, few things are sure.

Sister Joan Chittister writes, "The fear of loss, of change, of transition is the private nightmare of so many yet we see houses, even of the wealthy, washed away in rogue storms. We watch bank accounts wither. We see food lines lengthen. We hear of businesses that have closed, of professionals who have been overwhelmed with debt, of last year's secure, who have now become insecure. We fear, even in our security, the insecurity that stalks us all."

This stalking is why we toss and turn at night. Chittister goes on to say, "Certainty, for all of its guarantees, demands a subservient companion. It comes at the price of both liberty and creativity. It nails our feet to the floor and calls it success."

Making peace with insecurity or uncertainty looks like the continual surrendering that chapter 2 talks about, detaching from specific outcomes, and relying on the Spirit of God to comfort and teach us. We can also focus on being passionate about what we can control—things like having a plan for the risks involved in our decision, as well as how we love others and ourselves, how we engage with life's events, and how we move through the world.

Not only is asking questions of significance and breaking down mental roadblocks important as we consider particular pathways, there are a number of other ways we can test various possibilities.

I like to think of this part of the journey as filtering. It is similar to panning for gold. Since gold is heavier than other rocks, gold miners fill a metal pan with water and dirt and shake it. After a lot of shaking, the lighter rocks go away and the gold sinks to the bottom of the pan.

Like a miner, you can use the methods in this chapter to shake out your various choices and search for the decision that is most worthy.

*

When trying to discern whether to go up for tenure or quit my job, I meditated on two quotes for months. It's difficult to say precisely why.

I felt deep inside me that I was supposed to pay attention to these specific words. I was to read them and let them read me. I was to steep in their wisdom.

This first quote was from philosopher and spiritual advisor to Martin Luther King Jr., Howard Thurman. He said: "Don't ask what the world needs. Ask what makes you come alive and go do it. Because what the world needs is people who have come alive."

The other important words were part of a poem, "Sweet Darkness," by Anglo-Irish poet David Whyte.

> anything or anyone
> that does not bring you alive
> is too small for you.

A few months after beginning to pray over these words, I received an invitation to meet Father Richard Rohr. I was in Albuquerque where he lives, and a friend introduced us. Anyone familiar with Rohr's work would likely see his influence on my spirituality. His writing helped me to reconnect with the Bible, understand myself, and expand my understanding of God.

Like any of his many readers would be, I was amped to meet Fr. Rohr. He has written numerous best-selling books, but as a Franciscan friar dedicated to simplicity and generosity, he lives in a simple, small home in a church parking lot in the most underresourced part of Albuquerque.

He was everything I hoped—kind, present, humble, gracious, wise. In my view, he lives as he invites me to live. He practices what he preaches. He lives awake. I sat on a couch across from him, and roughly twenty minutes into the conversation, a piece of art hanging on the wall caught my attention.

It was Thurman's quote, in all of its glory.

The painting had a light and dark blue background and the words were in white. Both times the word "alive" was used, it was in the largest font. I told Fr. Rohr that I had been meditating on Thurman's words for months. Then he explained that people from around the world send him gifts of art, and so he switches out what's hanging in his living room every few months.

"This is hanging here just for you, Angela," he remarked, as tears welled up in my eyes.

A few weeks later, I received an email from someone that I had only met once. She wondered if our work might have some synergy, and she asked if I would read the introduction to her book. She had read my book on joy and integrated it into this section and wanted my thoughts.

I opened the document on my laptop. Near the top was a series of quotes, and as I scanned them, one stood out to me, of course.

"Anything or anyone that does not bring you alive is too small for you."

The same things were showing up in different places. I couldn't help but pay attention. This is synchronicity. It is not the only way to discern what to do, but it's helpful in your filtering process.

Are there particular themes, words, things, actions, or places that you have noticed several times over but in different spaces and times? Or have people from very different parts of your life said similar things?

When you notice the same things again and again, God might be trying to give you a sign of some sort. Perhaps God is showing you that it's the right time, or God is showing you a truth again and again until you confront it or accept it.

*

Another way you experience synchronicity is having the very thing you have been thinking about, needing or praying for mysteriously come to you. This kind of synchronicity can be evidence of God's provision or that your heart is aligned with what God wants.

Antony was an Egyptian, and his parents were both socially prominent and prosperous. One day he was walking to church and thought about various people before him, like the apostles who gave up everything they had to follow Jesus. He was also contemplating stories in the book of Acts in the Bible about people selling what they had and using the money to help others.

And seemingly, as God would have it, right when he walked into church, he heard a story being read about Jesus telling the rich man to sell everything he had and give it to the poor. He felt synchronicity in this moment. And immediately after leaving church, Antony began giving away possessions and selling other things and giving the money to people who were poor.

He then spent his life praying constantly and pursued a frugal life by himself in the wilderness for almost twenty years. Eventually when he came out, people were amazed by how healthy he was—physically and emotionally. He began reconciling friendships, consoling people who were mourning, and healing the sick. Over time, he persuaded many other people to take up the monastic life. And by the time of his death in 356 CE, he was known in Spain, Rome, and across North Africa.

He is now known as the father of monasticism, a way of living that influenced countless other people and informs the faith of many living today.

*

Another way of testing various possibilities is to consider the season of life you are currently in or are about to enter into.

What season is it? The writer of Ecclesiastes chapter 3 in the Hebrew Scriptures helps us to think about the different characteristics of seasons in our life.

Is it time to plant, to tend, to harvest, to let the ground lie fallow? What time are you in?

Is it time for separation? For healing? For rebuilding?

Is it time to weep or time to embrace the freedom of dancing and laughing?

God helps us to recognize the season we are in through a diverse array of signals—our energy level; recent experiences; responsibility for family and friends; mental, emotional, and physical capacities. If others in your community have a stake in your decision, their energy levels, etc., can be helpful signals.

Is it time to scatter what you have acquired—to share, to pass on, to set up a memorial to the good that has happened? Or is it time to gather, to take up something, to develop something, to learn, to build up, to refill?

Is it time to be alone or time to reach out and ask for what you need?

Are you in a season of hiddenness, a time to embrace unknowing and mystery? Or are you in a season of discovery, a time to embrace breakthroughs, insights, innovation, encounters?

Is it time to hold on or time to let go?

Thinking in terms of seasons helps us to realize that this decision is not the whole story. Each life includes many seasons.

Are you in a season marked by compassion or a season marked by moral anger?

Is it time to battle for what is right or to reconcile?

Perhaps read over this section again. Do any of the words above stand out to you? What resonates?

As you reflect on the season you are in, consider how your decision relates to the qualities of this time in your life. Does it make sense? Or is this season ending and your decision will help you to embrace the coming season?

*

You can also do some filtering by honoring how the different parts of you feel about each possible pathway. It is likely that you feel the struggle *within* as you imagine what to do. In other words, part of you wants to move in one direction while another part of you wants to move in a different direction.

Listen to the various parts of you. Name them. Is it stabilizer, responsible one, manager, firefighter, connector, pleaser, something else? Some of your parts may be younger versions of you—eight-year-old you that needed more care, fourteen-year-old you that needed to protect herself.

What is each part saying? What is each part reacting to? What does each part of you need?

Let them have a conversation with one another.

What do you learn as you listen to this conversation? As your higher wisdom listens in, what does she say?

If you can give the different parts of yourself what they need and think through what they are responding to, you can get clearer on which possibility is wisest. For example, if the firefighter within you feels afraid of potential chaos, you can take up a new habit that will calm your nervous system, like daily meditation. If the pleaser within you is concerned with losing a significant relationship, you can read the next chapter and get more insight into what to do if your decision risks relationships.

*

Ignatius of Loyola, whom you read about in the chapter "Surrendering," developed a helpful test for discerning whether we are moving in the right direction.

Are you moving toward God's presence or away?

When you are actively moving toward God's presence, you experience clarity and growth and feel the peace that passes understanding that the apostle Paul writes about. This peace is not always comfortable, as is clear in the stories of most people in this book; rather, it is a peace that is hard-won but mysteriously life-giving.

Even if your decision might challenge or disappoint others, it can still be moving toward God if it's moving toward something God values like peace or healing.

"There is a deeper voice of God, which we must learn to hear and obey. It will sound like the voice of risk, of trust, of surrender, of soul, of common sense, of destiny, of love, of an intimate stranger, of your deepest self. It will always feel gratuitous, and it is this very freedom that scares us. God never leads by guilt or shame!" explains Richard Rohr.

In this state of moving toward God, you will do things like restore balance, ignite your imagination, release positive energy, and direct your focus beyond yourself.

Shane Claiborne and his coauthors, in their book *Common Prayer*, put it this way: "The Scriptures tell us to 'test the spirits,' and the true test of the spirit of a thing is whether it moves us closer to God and to our suffering neighbor. Does it have fruit outside of our own good feelings?"

I'm struck by the types of encounters people had with Jesus. They were always moved toward some kind of freedom—freedom from unworthiness; freedom from narrow vision; freedom from being excluded or an outsider; freedom from worry and obsession with accumulation of things; freedom from mental and emotional torment; freedom from relational, spiritual, and physical distress; even freedom from abuse of power.

Jesus's encounter with Zacchaeus has stayed with me since I was a child. Zacchaeus is an outsider. He is disliked because tax collectors often took more than they should have from people. He has money, but it seems he has few friends.

He wants to see Jesus, but there is a crowd, and since he is short, he cannot see over other people, so he climbs a tree to get a glimpse of Jesus. Maybe I love this story because I am also petite!

Jesus notices Zacchaeus in the tree and goes to him and declares, "I must stay at your house today." Witnesses mutter to themselves in either disgust or frustration that Jesus has gone to be at the house of a man they do not respect or like.

Immediately Zacchaeus's life is changed by this brief encounter. He can't believe Jesus is coming to his house. He instantly vows to give away half of his money to the poor and to pay back four times whatever amount he has defrauded others. Jesus has not even gone to his house yet. The mere idea that this man, Jesus, that so many other people honor and love, wants to stay and dine with him frees him to relate to others in new ways.

The other story is about a woman whom I will call Maria who has been subjected to bleeding for twelve years. Twelve years! The woman is desperate for healing. Her condition has made her physically unwell, and it has also made her seem unclean to other people. Therefore, like Zacchaeus, she is likely feeling excluded and lonely.

In this story, there is another crowd of people pressing in on Jesus. Maria comes up behind Jesus and reaches out to touch the fringe of his clothes, and immediately her bleeding stops. Jesus notices that power has left him, so he asks who touched him. Of course, his closest friends are confused as to why he would ask this because he is surrounded by people.

Jesus persists.

Maria falls to the ground trembling before Jesus and explains why she touched him and how he healed her. Jesus calls her "Daughter," and tells her that her faith has made her well, and invites her to go in peace. She is free of her ailment and freed from how people have labeled her.

Anyone who leaves God's presence and continues in the same way—the rich man, for example—refuses God's freedom. The story of the rich man is the story Antony heard when he walked into the church and decided to become a monastic after experiencing synchronicity.

A rich man comes up to Jesus and calls him teacher and asks him what he must do to inherit eternal life. Initially, Jesus tells him to be faithful in his actions and keep the commandments, like not stealing.

The man says he has this covered and wants to know what else he lacks. Jesus tells him to sell all his possessions and give to the poor and to follow him. Suddenly, the man goes away sad because he has great wealth. He continues to live in bondage to his possessions and to a particular identity.

When you are moving away from God's presence and guidance, you feel divided, as if the steps you are taking are killing your spirit. You will experience things like resentment, fear, and selfishness. You will be drained of energy and might feel constrained, diminished, or confused. In this state we are often prone to self-pity, pettiness, blaming others, or being stingy.

Living in this state turns us inward, and we spiral into difficult feelings. It can cut us off from people who love us. It can also lessen our sense of the good—what God has done, how others have cared for us, the strength in us that has shown up, the beautiful things that have happened—and cloud our vision of the future. Any decision that involves the misuse of power or control, morose delight, superiority, arrogance, revenge, or a spirit of exclusion is not moving toward God.

*

Another form of filtering is pursuing the different possibilities or pathways in your mind to discern what might happen when you make various choices. Mental practice has been proven to be just as helpful to us as physical practice. For example, a study that examined golfers showed that those who combined physical practice together with mental practice (where they went through the motions of golf in their head) performed better than golfers who only underwent physical practice, even though both groups spent the same amount of time practicing overall.

So, go ahead and close your eyes and imagine going through all the motions and feelings for each path. Notice how you feel and what happens in your body. Are your muscles relaxed or tense? As you consider taking a particular path, do you have a knot in your stomach or feel like an elephant is on your chest? Or do you feel relief and release?

What unfolds before you as you live toward each choice? What kind of "fruit" might it cultivate—good things like patience or peace, or problematic things like resentment or a further divided life? Where does it lead? What do you think about where the path goes as you mentally imagine it?

Do the same thing with the challenges you have named. Imagine yourself navigating each challenge. What would you do? How would you respond effectively? What would it look like to overcome each challenge? What kind of "fruit" might it cultivate—good things like gentleness or joy, or problematic things like greed or discontent?

You can also mentally go through the best possible scenario and the worst possible scenario. What would each look like? If you were to fail or if things did not go well, what would you do next?

*

Sometimes God shows up as a kind of inner voice, an inner knowing.

During the eight months I wrestled with whether or not to leave my job, I posed important questions to trusted friends and family members. I prayed and read the Bible and other sacred texts. I met with my therapist. I reflected with colleagues. I created the discernment group I described in the chapter entitled "Seeking."

I cried. I got angry. I lamented. I got anxious and I released worry again and again. I reflected on who I am and who I am trying to become. I evaluated my deepest convictions and values. I saved money. I considered the financial implications of my decision.

I sought counsel from mentors and people it made sense to reach out to. I talked with people who stayed in academia, people who left, and those who were doing the kinds of things I wanted to do outside of higher education.

I imagined an alternative future. I opened myself up to numerous possibilities. I even applied to other jobs and was offered other positions. At the time, no job seemed quite right.

In the hustle of the waiting and from the blur of discerning, one day I heard clearly within me, "I have something different for you." And after months of discernment, this voice became the deciding factor for me.

Named United States poet laureate in 2019, Joy Harjo of the Muscogee Creek Nation writes compellingly about the role of "the knowing" in her life. In her memoir, *Crazy Brave*, she describes significant moments in her life when her knowing told her what to avoid and what to go toward.

Her stepfather was horribly abusive and terrifying, and she wanted to run away from home and was trying to figure out how to make this happen. At one point she was researching bus costs and considering sex work to support herself, which seemed like a better option than being sexually and physically abused by her stepfather.

Joy Harjo writes, "Though I was blurred with fear, I could still hear and feel the knowing. The knowing was my rudder, a shimmer of intelligent light, unerring in the midst of this destructive, terrible, and beautiful life. It is a strand of the divine, a pathway for the ancestors and teachers who love us."

The knowing gave her a sense of where this potential path would lead, and she realized it wouldn't be life-giving. But it didn't stop there. As she considered this path, instead of feeling free, she felt "a heaviness, a terrible grief."

Like Joy, as we imagine various possibilities and pay attention to our emotions and bodies, we will be led toward what to do and what not to do. "The knowing told me there was another way. The knowing always spoke wisely, softly," she explains.

Shortly after she realized she needed to find another way, she discovered information about an Indian boarding school. This led to a meeting, and as her mother was filling out the paperwork for this school, her mother mentioned her artwork. Suddenly the people at the agency were telling them both about an art institute for Native people that would not only be for high school but included two years in an undergraduate-level program.

As Joy held this brochure, a brightness filled her. She had previously associated the sun with God in her life and perceived this was divine guidance.

Joy was accepted, and as she made her way to the school, she felt strength, like she was headed in the right direction, and even felt inspired about her very life. The inner voice that channels God often speaks in a singular moment. Suddenly you can know this is the wrong path. Or: I am on the right path. I am heading toward a truth I must live.

*

Once you have direction, you can still ask God for confirmation that you are moving along the right path.

Gideon did this. He was a leader, a judge, and a prophet who was trying to figure out if he had heard correctly from God. He put out a fleece of wool overnight and asked God to put dew on the fleece only and to make the ground dry around it if he was going in the right direction. Gideon had a sense about what God wanted him to do and wanted God to confirm it.

In the morning, the fleece was covered in dew and the ground was dry.

But Gideon needed more confirmation. He put the fleece out once more and asked God not to be angry with him but to just help him out by making him double sure. This part of the story always makes me feel very seen!

This time Gideon asked that the fleece be dry but the ground around it be wet. As in, I'm not playing God. Give me a sign.

And in the morning the fleece was dry and the ground was wet. Just like he asked. Again.

We are free to be as bold as Gideon and bring our decisions to God and ask God to confirm it. Twice.

This confirmation could come in myriad forms—a peace that washes over you, the first good night's sleep you've had in months, a phone call or text, an email or a conversation showing up at just the right time.

If you don't have your own specific "fleece," simply ask God for any clear sign that will confirm for you that you are going in the right direction. You'll know if it comes.

And if you never see a kind of sign or confirmation, start going in the direction of your decision and see what happens in you or around you. Do you feel greater wholeness, love, joy, peace, goodness, truthfulness? Do you sense you are moving toward God?

FIELD NOTES TO SELF

- Ask questions informed by what matters most.
- Break down mental roadblocks by challenging and defining them.
- Filter and test various choices until you settle in your decision.

STRIVING

When Your Decision Risks Judgment, Hurt, and Relationships

A person who can see a little bit will resist guidance; a person who cannot see at all will stretch forth their hands and be led to unknown places where they don't know how to go.

—John of the Cross, *Dark Night of the Soul*

Peter Buxtun was twenty-seven years old in 1966, the year he was hired by Public Health Services in San Francisco to be a venereal disease investigator.

In the course of his work, he learned from colleagues about the Tuskegee experiment happening across the country in Alabama. Between 1932 and 1972, four hundred Black males with syphilis were monitored so investigators could learn about the effects of the disease on human bodies.

The participants had no idea they had an infectious disease and only enrolled because they were promised hot meals, free rides, and minor medical care like aspirin. "The infected group was simply told they had 'Bad Blood' that needed 'treatment by government doctors,'" explains Derek Kerr and Maria Rivero in their report for the Government Accountability Project.

This harmful experiment caused many other people to get infected—including the spouses and children of the men in the study—and many of those in the study died even though penicillin that could have saved their lives was widely available more than twenty years before the study was ended.

Understandably, Black Americans still struggle to trust medical professionals to this day because of this experiment. It confirmed their worst fears about medical racism.

When Buxtun first heard about this study, he was shocked. It was difficult to believe that an organization that was supposed to protect people did such horrifying harm.

Risking his job, career, and reputation, Buxtun decided to file a report that compared what was happening to the Nazi physicians who experimented on people imprisoned at concentration camps. When he showed the report to his boss, his boss said, "When they come to fire you, or whatever they're going to do, forget my name. I've got a wife and kids. I want to keep my job."

Peter was brought to headquarters in Atlanta and confronted by colleagues who were angry at his report. They wanted to intimidate him into leaving or staying quiet. He refused both.

Others also tried to protest what was happening, but no one more than Buxtun, who spent multiple years trying to shut down the study.

Even after he left his job with the Public Health Service for law school, Buxtun leaked information on the Tuskegee experiment to the press. Eventually, it made the front page of the *New York Times*, and the study was finally terminated. Before Tuskegee, there were no federal guidelines to protect research subjects.

There is a kind of negative peace that Buxtun refused. Sometimes we believe that preserving peace by doing nothing, ignoring a problem, compromising for the sake of fake harmony is actual peace. It is not. To keep the peace by turning a blind eye to unethical behavior or by ignoring doing what is right or what we know is ours to do is negative peace.

Peacebuilders know that sometimes working toward actual peace requires risking reputation, status, understanding, judgment, hurt, and disappointment.

> *Question: What if?*
> *Prayer: Encourage me.*

Imagine a graph. On one axis is how close you are to someone versus distance in the relationship. On another axis is how shame-free to how closed-down you are in the relationship.

If you are not close to someone and find yourself quite closed-down when talking to them, it is wise to be careful about how much of your decision-making journey you invite them into. On the other hand, you may be quite close to someone and also find yourself quite closed-down when talking with them.

It is better for our souls to discuss the most intimate details of difficult decisions with people we feel both close to *and* nearly shameless around.

People tend to fall into four categories: supporting, prying, asserting, ghosting. You may not encounter all of these types, though. It depends on how complex your decision is and whether it involves others.

Some people in your life will support you by answering the phone when you call; joining your discernment group; asking open-ended, curious questions out of concern and love; praying for you; helping you count the costs and name the risks; giving loving advice; and encouraging you along the way. They may even offer some challenging or uncomfortable words, but you will know they are coming from a place of deep respect and affection for you.

They will lift you up on the days you need it most, have coffee with you, take you in if you need a place to stay, cook you a meal while you process, text with you incessantly as you mull over every aspect of your decision.

While your decision might be disorienting for supportive people in your life, especially those who have or would have made a different decision, overall, you will sense that they trust you are being thoughtful and careful, and listening for God's guidance.

Prying people, on the other hand, insert themselves into your decision-making process even though they do not know you well, you have not sought them out, and they are not an expert in what you are processing.

These types of people may try to press you into sharing details you don't want to share or giving advice that you haven't asked for. They could also make you feel pressured to defend or explain your decision.

When I think about people in the Bible that made bold decisions, I am struck by the lack of recorded conversations in which they explain themselves to others. They ask for help, prayer, fasting, solidarity, but they don't first beg people to understand where they are coming from or try to justify their decisions. They are Miriam, Abraham, Joseph, Esther, Daniel, Deborah, Mary, Peter, Paul, and Jesus, just to name a few.

Assume that at least one or two prying people will take your decision and make it about them.

"Oh, you don't drink? Let me tell you the ten reasons alcohol isn't a problem in my life."

"Oh, you're in a time of 'deconstructing.' Let me tell you why I think this is trending and not a good thing."

"Oh, you're not in a relationship with them anymore? Let me tell you why I don't give up on other people and forgive and forget."

"Oh, you're thinking of retiring. Let me explain why I could never just sit and watch TV all day."

"Oh, your boss is controlling. Let me tell you how I ignore my work conditions by focusing on how meaningful my work is."

Human beings pay such close attention to other people's lives, deciding what we think about how others live, because we are usually wondering, "Should I live that way too?" Or we are reacting, "I could not live that way. It's not for me." Essentially, other people's judgments about us are really judgments about themselves—about what they believe, value, like, dislike, want to do, or never would want to do. Especially when they don't know us or haven't listened to us well.

There may also be assertive types who punch you in the gut with their criticism. They write long emails or texts or give drawn-out monologues about what they think you should do or should have done. They question things like your judgment, sanity, wisdom, purity and holiness, love, as well as your reputation, goals, and commitment.

Sometimes people will be deeply saddened about your decision and, instead of lamenting constructively, they will take it out on you.

Additionally, any protesting of the status quo, the abusive religious community, the unhealthy relationship, the toxic work environment, the long-held expectations or beliefs, invites others to examine their own lives. Some people will welcome that opportunity. Others will resist it.

The prying and asserting hurt. A primary way we survive as social creatures is acceptance of our peers, coworkers, friends, and family. And their judgment is painful enough that we can avoid making decisions we know are likely to draw negative attention.

You may be feeling that this decision is risking a relationship or several. There could even be people who ghost you. They could disappear instantly without warning or conversation or allow a slow separation. It's a form of marginalizing you or the people involved in your decision.

Here are a few of the many good reasons you might risk a relationship or risk being ghosted (or even risk ending a relationship).

You love peace more than chaos.
You are not emotionally or mentally equipped to keep going in the same direction.
You do not feel seen or heard.

You tried to improve the relationship and, even after exhausting all
paths, nothing improved.

You want to be emotionally and mentally well, and the relationship
does not support that.

You tried implementing boundaries, and they were not respected.

You have accepted who the other person is, and the relationship does
not allow you to be who you are.

You have decided you should no longer tolerate the other person's
actions.

There is a kind of trust fall that happens when we make a decision
that risks relationships. It is a trust that some people that truly love
us will catch us, or that others we have not yet connected with will
eventually catch us.

It is to trust that when we feel weak, God's strength carries us. It
is to trust that with God's help, we can deal with any outcome with
integrity, courage, love.

It means trusting God and the cast of people in it with the story
of our life.

＊

If you make a choice that surprises other people, goes against the grain, or
disrupts people's expectations, you should anticipate awkward or hurtful moments with your family, friends, coworkers, even strangers.

Right now, you can make a plan.

Imagine different types of encounters and walk yourself through
what you will do. Recall that mental practice is just as powerful as
actually practicing something.

A few things to consider while you're preparing for challenging
conversations:

- Whenever you feel the need to respond to someone, pause and
ask yourself, "Is my need to respond coming from a place of

shame, blame, accusation, guilt, fear? Will this be fruitful? Do I
have the emotional and mental capacity to respond right now?" If
not, what are you willing to talk about? Start talking about that—
be it the weather, a question for them, your upcoming vacation,
or the meeting you need to get to.

- Decide how close to and shame-free you feel around this person
  and whether it is wise to engage in conversation or not. If not,
  it's best to create a boundary and share it in a clear, concise way.
  Something like, "I hear what you are saying, but I would prefer
  not to talk about it." Or, "I know you would like to have your
  questions answered or to share your thoughts, but I am not ready
  to have this conversation. I don't know if I ever will be."

- If you want to talk with a specific person about your decision and
  know it will be hard, decide what aspects of your decision you
  want to share. If your decision impacted them, decide now what
  kind of difficult feelings you will address and who you are willing
  to apologize to. Limit the time ahead of time by having it online
  or having another commitment after the conversation.

- If it feels right to you, tell prying or asserting people how they
  can show you love and respect. After my divorce, I told someone who was being very judgmental, "This is already really hard.
  Please stop what you're saying or I need to end this conversation.
  I would really appreciate support of some kind instead."

Above all, guard your heart. It is the wellspring of your life, after
all.

*

It is wildly hard to look into the faces of people we love and tell them
something that is going to change the way they spend their time, their
holidays, their relationships.

It is one thing to make a difficult decision that changes our life,
and another to do so in a way that changes the lives of others. For

some of you, part of your journey in making your decision requires reflecting on the various possibilities going forward in light of others in your life.

And it is not just if you are considering a change in a close relationship. If you are considering a work transition or thinking about leaving a community or making medical decisions, you too are trying to reflect on how your choice will impact others.

We struggle to make hard decisions not just because we fear judgment, but because we fear disappointing people we care about.

On top of these things, many of us want to be seen as good. If we make decisions that other people don't understand or approve of, they may see us in a different light. It can be extremely painful. To actively disappoint people or go against what others want or open ourselves to people questioning our goodness requires a deep, abiding commitment within to our higher wisdom.

Letting go of the need for other people to understand our why in difficult decisions (which is also our desire for people to believe we made the right decision given the circumstances) is perhaps the hardest thing of all.

Some of the most important work on this journey is the inner work you have been doing along the way—learning acceptance, expressing difficult feelings, recalling important stories that have shaped you, shedding story lines, reckoning with your beliefs, discerning what values should guide you—that will make you capable of letting other people down for the sake of something you think matters more.

It is easiest to make a decision that involves disruption, conflict, and risk when we realize *not* choosing something means compromising our integrity, wholeness, love.

This is another time in this journey when you can lean into acceptance. Accept that you are loved unconditionally and accept that you may need to disappoint other people on your journey. Hopefully, they will one day come to their own understanding about your decision. Hopefully, one day they will come to see that the choice you made was about a deeply held value, a thing you couldn't not do. Whether they do or not is not yours to manage.

*

What are you responsible for?

It may be helpful to imagine "property lines" around your decision. If you own a house or land, there are imaginary lines around it that divide what is yours from what is someone else's. In the case of your decision, where do the property lines begin and end? What is truly yours, and what is someone else's to own?

You can do a lot of things to consider the consequences of your various pathways, but at the end of the day you cannot manage the future. You are not that powerful. You cannot completely control outcomes. You can be prudent, but you cannot predict everything that will happen as a result of your decision.

You can do things with great love, integrity, intention, compassion, and hope, and you can make the best decision you know how to make with the information you have.

You are not responsible for how other people respond or react to your decision. Other people's feelings, beliefs, values, issues, fear of the future, desires, and habits are theirs. And yours are yours.

It is really tough to apply this to children because they generally have so little power in what is happening around them, but you can't control how they respond, protect them from having difficult feelings, or prevent them from facing any struggle.

You can help them constructively work through their emotions using the chapter entitled "Sensing," and you can get them a counselor or mentor and pastoral care. You can regularly talk about what is happening and hear how it's impacting them and empathize with them. You can love them well. And you can shed anything that is holding you back from moving forward. You can forgive yourself, and you can forgive others. You can model what surrender, trust, and faith look like.

*

When you lose something massive—a significant relationship, your sense of your identity, your physical health, your religious community, your marriage, your job—you need a purposeful plan for recovery and restoration.

Here are a few ideas to help you create your recovery plan:

- Do the "museum of your life" exercise in the appendix regularly (it's related to the chapter "Summoning").
- Learn how to do something new that can help you see yourself in a new light, nurture confidence, and expand your sense of self: cooking, dance classes, pickleball, watercolor painting, playing a musical instrument, studying a new language.
- Use an app like Meetup or a social media platform to gather in person or online with people who are in a similar season.
- Join a grief group. Use the chapter "Sensing" to continually work through difficult feelings.
- Read about real self-care in the book by Pooja Lakshmin (see note) and continue to do meaningful internal work that will sustain you.
- Schedule time with friends and family in advance. Create a calendar of whom you will call or meet up with each week. If you do this a month at a time, you will have people to connect with, which is so healing, even on the days you feel really down.
- Ask for help when you need it. Tell people when you need their prayers and encouragement or to share a meal.
- Find a therapist, spiritual director, chaplain, or clergyperson to meet with.
- Expect ebbs and flows. There will be days that you feel really positive and hopeful, and there could be days when you ruminate or question yourself or simply miss what was.

*

Anna May Wong was born in Los Angeles in 1905. She was the first Chinese American to become a movie star in Hollywood. "She introduced the American public to a compelling vision of Chinese American and Asian American identity," writes biographer Katie Gee Salisbury.

While growing up, Anna May spent most of her time at the Chinese Mission School or her dad's laundry business, but one day she was captivated by seeing people acting in the streets of Chinatown in Los Angeles. Suddenly, visiting film sets and watching movies was all she wanted to do. She became known as the Curious Chinese Child on sets around Chinatown.

Anna May spent her life dedicated to acting despite disappointing people and experiencing deep hurt and judgment. She always helped out with the family business, but she had no interest in learning domestic handicrafts in order to be the right kind of Chinese wife or pursuing work that her family thought she should seek. In fact, when she first told her parents she wanted to be an actress they "hit the ceiling." At the time, her parents believed actors were among the lowest ranks of Chinese society. But Anna May defended her dream and herself and went on to star in multiple films and TV series.

Frustratingly, she was constantly typecasted and endured harmful racism. Also, roles that should have been played by Asian women were given to women who were not Asian even though she and other women like her were more than capable. One of the hardest decisions she made was to turn down a minor role in a major film, *The Good Earth*, that eventually won two academy awards. Explaining her reasoning she said, "If you let me play O-lan, I'll be very glad. But you're asking me—with Chinese blood—to do the only unsympathetic role in a picture featuring an all American cast portraying Chinese characters." The leads in the film were going to be white actors in makeup. She took a huge risk by rejecting this role publicly and explaining why what was happening was wrong.

This decision was pivotal. "Anna May got to thinking: in almost two decades of working in the movies, she had bent and bowed to the demands of Hollywood, no matter how absurd or dismissive the requests," writes Salisbury. Anna May's desire to be an actress meant she had taken whatever was offered and often directors didn't even tell her what she was signing up to do until she was in front of the camera.

Her decision to reject the role in *The Good Earth* changed the trajectory of her career. Anna May decided to no longer play roles that cast a negative image of China and the Chinese. She took other risks throughout her life, always advocating for what she believed in, valued, and felt called toward over what people thought of her.

Over a century after she was born, she became the first Asian American to have her image put on United States quarters. "The very same coins she once used to buy tickets at the movie theater now feature her indelible face, blunt-cut bangs and all," reflects Salisbury. Her legacy and spirit live on in the many other actors and movie viewers that she has influenced and inspired.

As I have reviewed people throughout history for this book— Jackie Robinson, Dolores Huerta, Amma Syncletica, and Anna May Wong—who lost one form of belonging, I have noticed they eventually gained another kind of belonging. And it was truer, freer, deeper, worthier.

It was a kind of belonging that did not cost them their very soul. In fact, it was a kind of belonging that demanded them to be exactly who they were created to be.

FIELD NOTES TO SELF

- Anticipate challenging conversations.
- Trust the journey you have been on and your ability to make the right decision.
- Make a restoration plan.

SATED JOY

When You Want to Keep Moving Forward

A joy that does not hunger for more and more, but rests, satisfied.

—Paul Kalanithi, *When Breath Becomes Air*

There was a point in the third century when the Roman emperor Septimius Severus prohibited people from converting to Christianity or Judaism. When the governor of Carthage enforced this edict, a woman named Perpetua and four others who were preparing for baptism were arrested and condemned to death in the arena. Another Christian voluntarily joined them.

At the time, Perpetua was twenty-two years old and had a baby that she was still breast-feeding. Her former slave, Felicity, who had become her friend, was pregnant when she was also arrested.

Perpetua writes about how her father tried multiple times, first in anger and then in great sadness, and then from a point of devastation, to get Perpetua to renounce her faith. But she remained steadfast, explaining that she could not disavow her Christianity because it was who she was.

Once she was in prison, she confessed to being terrified for herself and overwhelmed with worry for her baby. At one point, she was able to arrange for her baby to stay with her in prison, but eventually her baby was taken from her by her family. Her father tried to use her baby to convince her to change her mind and stay alive.

Perpetua had several visions while she was in prison. Each one showed her suffering followed by a kind of victory. Through these visions, she felt God was preparing her for her death and that she could accept it, knowing that God would welcome her into the life to come.

Felicity gave birth to a baby girl in prison two days before she was to be martyred.

All six people were paraded from prison to an amphitheater to participate in "the games," and it was reported that they all did so joyously. Perpetua's face was shining and her steps were calm and she was singing a hymn. Felicity was rejoicing that she had safely given birth. They kissed each other as a ritual of peace right before dying. To the end, they were committed to their faith and to their love for one another.

Perpetua journaled about her trial and imprisonment, and it's one of the rare documents we still have written by a woman in the ancient world. Perpetua's journal was so influential that it was read every year in Carthage's churches for centuries.

Most of us will never confront a decision as painful as Perpetua and Felicity's. But there is something we can all gain from reflecting on the sated joy that they welcomed in the midst of their incredibly challenging decisions.

> *Question: How do I live into my story?*
> *Prayer: Thank you.*

Sometimes you come to know the thing you need to do but don't want to do it because you know it will break your heart. Maybe it will break someone else's heart too. It is one thing to ask God for what to do, and another to pray to have the strength to do it when you know what you need to do.

When we are making a decision that hurts, we are often choosing between familiar and unfamiliar pain. We are choosing between a pain we have ways of managing and a pain we are unsure how to treat. And most of us favor pain we already know how to manage.

As Michaela O'Donnell Long, author and executive director of Fuller Seminary's Max De Pree Center for Leadership, helped me to understand, sometimes we are also choosing between a dull ache that we have learned to live with and a gut-wrenching pain that seems unbearable. Most of us prefer chronic pain over acute pain.

*

Dorothy Day knows about decisions that ache. Day is famous for helping to birth the Catholic Worker Movement by opening "houses of hospitality" for people who needed something to eat and somewhere to stay. Today you can find Catholic Worker houses and associated ministries across the country and world.

Day is much less famous for what she gave up to be able to do this work.

For years, she experienced the dull ache of not doing something she felt called to do. She wanted to convert to Catholicism and, with her conversion, commit her life to solving societal problems that keep people poor, hungry, and sick.

"Even before the Great Depression, Day had been sensitive to the plight of the poor, a sensitivity that ultimately shaped her calling," explains Casey Cep in an article about her radical faith.

The thing is, in order to follow this sacred call that she felt she had, she needed to give up her common-law marriage because her partner was a dedicated anarchist who was not religious and refused to be married in a church or legally. Day loved this person deeply. She adored their partnership.

She tried at times to do both, to remain in her marriage and to pursue a life beyond her relationship that involved participating in movements for change. But she felt disconnected from God and the faith she was supposed to live out. She realized she needed to choose between the man she loved and God. She writes, "I wanted to die in order to live.... I wanted to be united to my love." And the love she was speaking of was an ultimate, decisive love for the church, for Christ.

Though Day went on to create an extraordinary movement that impacted people experiencing poverty for generations, she did so at the cost of her own happiness for a significant amount of time. "I never regretted for one minute the step which I had taken in becoming a Catholic, but I repeat that for a year there was little joy for me as the struggle continued," she explains in her aptly titled memoir, *The Long Loneliness*.

In order to pursue what you believe is worthy, you might need to sacrifice your own happiness, at least for a time. You might need to give yourself over to acute, unfamiliar pain to eventually settle your spirit, find inner peace, follow where you know you are being led.

Parker Palmer explains it this way, "Where do people find the courage to live divided no more when they know they will be punished for it? The answer I have seen in the lives of people like Dorothy Day is simple: these people have transformed the notion of punishment itself. They have come to understand that no punishment anyone might inflict on them could possibly be worse than the punishment they inflict on themselves by conspiring in their own diminishment."

*

We want so much for God to whisper into our ears, or maybe even better, fly a little airplane across the sky with a banner that reads "Choose this. Everything will be all right if you take this path."

My friend David Gist calls this "obvious God." I prefer obvious God.

But even if it seems God is speaking clearly, we must always speak about God's will with humility. Because sometimes we believe

God told us something, and later we realize we made a mistake. Sometimes we do and say things because we think God told us to, and we are wrong. So anytime we look for God and try to join God in what God is doing, anytime we think God has shown up and shown us the way, we do so with the understanding that we could be misguided.

Wisdom is a journey, not a destination.

The three books in the Bible that discuss God's wisdom, living wisely, and nurturing wisdom—Proverbs, Ecclesiastes, and Job—*all* say that wisdom begins with a "fear of the Lord," which means great humility and total dependence and trust in God.

Even as we live with the possibility of making mistakes, miraculously we are caught up in the goodness of God and the universe. God's character does not change, and God's view of us does not change even if we mess up. *When* we mess up.

God wants good things for human beings—you included—and leads us toward the good. This doesn't mean life always feels good or even appears good, and it doesn't mean every choice we make is good.

Rather, it all miraculously comes together—the broken relationships, the gut-wrenching career choices, the beautiful intimate moments, the life-changing revelations, the challenging conversations, the hard-won wisdom, the crucible experiences—this thing and that thing and, yes, somehow even that thing—at the end, it all meets in God's ultimate good.

Nothing is wasted.

Not because God wants us to experience heartbreak, but because God's love and grace always transform, resurrect, heal.

*

I thought I was going to toss my cookies all over the seat.

I had taken Dramamine, but it was overmatched by the winding mountain road and large bus I was riding in. Finally, we turned into a parking lot, and I could get off the bus. Lucky for me, the moment I stepped off, I looked out and the incredible landscape captivated me so much that I nearly forgot how sick I felt.

I had made it to the place where Ignatius of Loyola prayed and eventually gave up his sword, dagger, and dagger belt (a story in chapter 2, "Surrendering").

Montserrat, with its pointy, picturesque mountain peaks, has a sidewalk that goes along a huge cliff. You look down from the top, and you remember how small you are, in the best kind of way. This is the place where Ignatius had made one of his biggest and likely most difficult decisions of his life.

You can see for miles, and there are other mountains nearby, covered in glorious green trees. As you take the path upward, you eventually discover the buildings that house the pilgrims who journey to this sight, the monastery, and the church.

In order to go into the sanctuary of the church, you walk through a courtyard with gigantic walls on all sides of you but no ceiling. So you naturally look up into the sky. It creates a holy place in time where it feels like you can touch God or, better yet, God can touch you.

I made my way into the sanctuary eager to see the Black Madonna that Ignatius and so many other pilgrims had visited over the centuries, only to be initially disappointed.

The Black Madonna sits high above the central altar encased in glass, and it is very difficult to see her from a distance. So of course, I asked what it took to get closer to her and discovered there is a special line you can get in where you can get right in front of her and even touch her if you want to.

I didn't come to Spain to see her from hundreds of feet away, so I was willing to wait. The path through the church to get to the Black Madonna is itself exceptional and sacred. On the way there, you walk past chapels, small rooms to the side of the sanctuary.

One is dedicated to Ignatius. There is a painting of him in a black robe on his knees with hands outstretched looking up at Jesus.

As you continue past the small chapels, you encounter a wall of white stone with intricate figures of angels and children cut into it. There was something interesting and beautiful to me about being welcomed into this space by angels and children. If we let them, they can both be guides.

This wall is the entrance to a small set of stairs. As you climb the stairs, you notice they are lined with colorful mosaics of saints of the Christian tradition, all females. What a sight to behold—Perpetua and Monica, to name just two.

I felt mysteriously connected to these women. The past twenty-two years of difficulty as a woman in ministry and theology walked up the stairs with me. It was another reminder of the way my story is caught up in the stories of countless others.

So much of life screams that we are alone. This small stairwell was a memorial to the fact that we are not.

I made my way up one more small set of stairs and saw her from the side initially. There she was, her dark beautiful face and body dripping in gold.

This Black Madonna has a smaller statue of Jesus on her lap. Other than their Black faces, they are covered in gold headdresses and garments. Her hands are out, the right one holds a gold ball; this is the only part of the two statues you can touch. The glass around them has a cutout just for her hand.

Many people say a prayer or lovingly look at her during their brief visit before walking down another stairwell and into a small chapel behind her. Like so many other pilgrims who have visited, I touched her hand. I began to pray as I stood in front of her—"God, grant me wisdom. God, lead me. Please give me discernment, God."

*

Until I ended up in a church parking lot making the hardest phone call of my life, I had never prayed in front of a likeness of Mary. I had heard of Ignatius and his spiritual exercises that help people make decisions, but until I studied his life for this book, I didn't know he had surrendered his sword in front of a statue of Mary.

As I reflect on the role Mary has played in my life during the last few years, I am not surprised that God would use her to comfort, guide, and heal me.

I needed to see God in new ways. I needed to know the God who saw, chose, and loved Mary.

Mary was young, poor, and all-around unremarkable before she became Jesus's mother. And none of those things lessened her in God's eyes.

Mary is a metaphor for me, for us. We are Mary. Mary is us.

Whatever our age, our gender, our socioeconomic standing, however common we are, God can surprise us with new vision, audacious love, and gratuitous grace.

I needed to see how God led Mary toward a future she didn't seek out. I needed to notice how God sustained her.

Mary knows about total dependence on God. If we let her, she shows us the way.

It was Mary's incredible, wild, precious *yes* that birthed the incarnation. As Fr. Richard Rohr says, "Mary is the model of the faith to which God calls all of us: a total and unreserved yes to God's request to be present in and to the world through us." Her decision to be the mother of God was complex. At times, it filled her with awe-inspiring joy. But as the months and years went by, that decision was also the source of deep pain.

Mary was likely judged since she was unmarried and pregnant, and then her son grew up to be one who was judged, threatened, and misunderstood, and he ultimately died young.

Her decision to be the mother of God meant her heart knew the intermingling of joy and sorrow intimately.

Difficult decisions often fuse sorrow and joy. Whether we stay or go, start or stop, boldly say yes or boldly say no, keep going or transition, detach or reconcile, gather or release, let it be or let it go, take up something or release something to die, we know what it is to feel simultaneously hallowed sorrow and sobering joy.

There is always a path we didn't take, a possibility we didn't pursue. And, generally, making a difficult decision involves grieving what was or what could have been or never will be. To decide also means gaining and wholeheartedly walking in a particular direction. It's a mix of grief and peace.

To feel both simultaneously—sorrow and joy—*is* a sign that you are deeply human. It is a sign that you live aware of life's brokenness and loss, and also aware of life's ability to astonish you with awe.

Your heart isn't broken when you feel sorrow mingled with your joy. Your heart is working. It is doing its job.

What you might have already discovered or will soon discover is that no matter what you actually decide, your journey to that decision offers an awakening. You cannot go on a journey related to a crossroads, a conflict, a crisis, or a crucible and not be different afterward.

Something new has emerged. How has your story transformed on this journey? What new story line or theme might you take up?

As you embrace what you have discovered about yourself, others, your life, the world, remember that beautiful and brutal saying that new wine cannot fit into old wineskins.

Wineskins were made of leathered animal skin and used in the past to store wine. At one point during his ministry, Jesus reminds listeners that if they pour new wine into old wineskins, they will burst and the wine and wineskins will be ruined. All this to say, you can't just go back to the way things were before this journey.

What do you need to do to protect what has emerged? What are the old wineskins? Better yet, what are the new ones?

*

The church in Montserrat was built right next to caves that are believed, like the Black Madonna, to be sources of healing that God uses. This is why there are ledges where people can pray and place lit candles in the shallow caves just outside of the church walls.

There is one large candle, about three feet tall, that remains lit at all times near the boxes of candles that people can choose from. Everyone uses this big candle to light theirs before placing them in a cave.

This tall candle is formed each night by the wax of the candles that are still burning on the ledges of the caves. The monks who live in the abbey gather all the burning candles and pour the hot wax all together into this large candle each evening.

When you light your candle to say your prayer, you do so on the prayers of countless other pilgrims who have made their way to this same place.

I chose a candle and started praying as I lit it. I held it for a couple of minutes and continued to pray until I found a special place to put it. I chose a spot underneath Torre De David, thinking of my dad, David, who died several years ago. I imagined him as a protector of my prayers.

I shook my head in near disbelief when I later learned that Mary is known as the Torre De David or Tower of David because of how she constantly defended her son, Jesus.

*

As I tapped the keys on the keyboard, my mind churned faster than I could type. I thought of everything that had been revealed to me during my discernment journey.

I imagined how my letter of resignation would be received, how surprised people would be, and what I would say after people had read it. It was a hard letter to write. It required saying uncomfortable things and sharing vulnerable feelings and thoughts.

More than anything, it meant going from an insider to being an outsider. Instantly. One minute I was writing this letter and had a title, an office door with my name on it, a clear professional trajectory, a legible story about who I am in the world.

When I pressed send, all that vanished. And I had no way of knowing how everything would shake out over the coming months or what the next year would hold.

The response to my letter was agonizing for someone who had just spent a decade collecting accolades. Virtual silence from my former employer. I cleaned out my office by myself and left my key and laptop and that was it.

Thankfully, I did have an informal community at that institution that took it upon themselves to send me off with one of the most heartfelt, beautiful evenings of my life. I will always remember it. That night was just one extension of the love and grace of God that have sustained me.

I am freer today than I have been in a long time. And I get to do work every day that matters deeply to me—speaking, writing, and consulting about things that keep people awake at night.

There have been days since leaving, as there were in the days after my divorce, in which I have wrestled with grief, sadness, and anger. After we walk through fire, we know more—about ourselves, about others, about how the world works, about all of it smashed together.

It can be heavy.

If you struggle with regret, try to pinpoint it. What is the thing or what are the few things that you are ruminating on? You are recycling something in your mind for a reason. Go back to where this journey started. Notice what is stirring.

Surrender it.

Shed it.

You can only move forward. You can't go back, so there is no point in playing certain scenes on repeat. As you think of the past that you are struggling not to dwell in, consider what you learned. How are you different because of what you've lived through? Focus on that.

"Letting go has consequences. Finally, the striving is over, the effort to salvage and fix, be or do something, is over. It is as if we have been clinging to the wall of a mountain of our own making, a mountain of expectations, striving, and goals. When that mountain disappears, we plummet.... When we let go, the only constants are God's love and God's promise that we will never be left alone," writes Barbara Holmes.

Take that with you into tomorrow.

There have also been countless days during recent years that I have marveled at the goodness I am constantly encountering, had resources to say yes to things that have made my life so much fuller, and been filled with that peace that passes understanding.

*

The team of young men who moved all of my heavy furniture and nearly twenty-five boxes of books frantically grabbed the last few items.

The sky had grown dark, and we could hear thunder in the distance. They rushed around the house I had just sold making sure every room was empty. One of the men closed the doors to the Pod while the other two looked up into the sky and cheered as they talked about the rain that was coming. They had already planned to go fishing the next morning, and they said the rain helps the fish to get hungry and bite.

The wind blew and the clouds moved wildly across the sky. It hadn't rained in Texas in weeks. My grass was brown and dead.

I went inside and cleaned my kitchen counters and my fridge. I grabbed the final odds and ends from around the house and put the bags of garbage near the front door. I took the cleaning supplies to my car. I came back in, grabbed the last two bags and locked the front door.

As I walked outside, it began to sprinkle. Water hit my face and arms. And as I got into the driver's seat of my car, the sky opened and rain poured down.

Anyone who knows me well—or has read my book *The Gravity of Joy*—knows rain makes me think of change. And God.

"Change is coming," I thought, shaking my head at the synchronicity of it all. And also, "Oh God, you are so good to me. You have me. You have my back, like you always have."

I called two of my dearest friends, Sarah and Anne, who lived near me and know what rain means to me. They both also knew I was moving out of my house that day.

Anne said she thought of me right when she realized it was going to rain and said, "This is God's signature to you." It was impossible not to be filled with awe, with the quiet, transformative joy that comes with meaningful transitions despite pain.

*

As God and the universe would have it, I booked a hotel room to go to after packing the Pod that was near the church where I had called my former husband to talk to him about divorce a year and a half earlier.

I didn't realize it until the next morning when I was getting coffee at Starbucks. I was driving through the same parking lot that I had gone through that day trying to find a spot to call him.

Suddenly, I realized where I was and knew what I needed to do. I parked my car in the church parking lot once more and walked into the sanctuary.

There she was, the statue of Mary, dimly lit by glowing candles on both sides of her.

I knelt before Mary again.

I thanked her for sustaining the life of God and for being a friend and guide that I couldn't have known how much I needed. I expressed gratitude to God for all that I have learned about myself—both the hard things and the good things—and about others, and about the world after making my two wildly difficult decisions.

I praised God for all that God had led me through since my divorce and resignation. I prayed for my former husband and for other people whose lives were impacted by the weighty decisions of the last few years. I talked with God about the hope I felt for all that is to come and for the courage I need to keep moving forward. To keep making hard decisions.

Sated Joy

*

Good decisions, bad decisions, mediocre decisions. God loves us. God is with you always and everywhere.

God is trustworthy.

You are trustworthy.

In *When Breath Becomes Air*, author Paul Kalanithi describes what it is like to be nearly finished with a decade of training as a neurosurgeon and to suddenly be diagnosed with stage IV lung cancer. There is a moment in his brilliant memoir that stunned me. He is holding his infant, Cady. He knows he is close to death. Life and death are intertwined.

Tenderly, he believes there is only one thing to say to this little one that he loves dearly. He writes that he wants her to know she has "filled a dying man's days with a sated joy, a joy that does not hunger for more and more, but rests, satisfied."

Let that wash over you.

When the time comes for you to embrace the new chapter in your story, I hope you are filled with a sated joy.

I hope that for just a few minutes—longer if you can let it—you will give yourself over to this wondrous joy that is the result of a recognition that right here, right now, you are centered, undivided, that what is, is enough.

It's okay if the big picture still feels overwhelming. Focus on just one aspect of this moment. Consider the wholeness, integrity, mindfulness, presence, health, love, or peace that you are cultivating with God's help. Look at it with amazement. Be in awe of the stories you have lived, surrendered, summoned, shed.

Marvel at the way you have endured. You were brave enough to take this journey. And you can revisit its lessons throughout your life whenever you have another tough decision to make.

Marvel at the ways the universe has held you.

Marvel at the fact that your story is caught up in the stories of others living and dead, and their courage, their wisdom, their healing, their love is within you.

Marvel that you participate in the Great Story.
This is an end. It's also a beginning.

FIELD NOTES TO SELF

- Nothing is wasted.
- When you experience sorrow and joy at the same time, your heart is working.
- No matter what you choose, you are loved.

APPENDIX:
THINGS TO DO TO HELP
YOU DECIDE WHAT TO DO

For downloadable versions of these activities, visit www.angelagorrell.com.

CHAPTER 1: STIRRING

Use the iceberg exercise to help yourself or a group explore the complexities and nuances of a difficult issue.

On a piece of paper, draw an iceberg floating in water. When drawing your iceberg, try to take up the whole page so you can write words onto the iceberg both above the waterline and below the waterline. Look up images of icebergs online if you want inspiration.

A floating iceberg has a portion of its ice that can be seen *above the water*. This is the part that is obvious to people who are looking at it. In the part of your iceberg above the water, write the issue you are dealing with as you see it.

A floating iceberg often has much more ice *under the water*. When it comes to your situation, what is "beneath the surface" for you?

1. What all are you feeling? Sadness? Anger? Fear? Surprise? Curiosity? Interest? You can feel pleasurable feelings and difficult feelings at the same time. If you are having trouble naming your feelings, write something about that.

2. Consider your past and how it might be impacting how you are experiencing this decision. Write what parts of your past are weighing on you.

3. What convictions of yours are bumping against each other as you consider this decision? Write down the beliefs, using the word "and" to explore what may be colliding within you. Example: I believe forgiveness is essential *and* I believe boundaries are essential.

4. What values are at play in this decision? Write down the values, using the word "and" to explore what values you feel like you may need to choose between. Example: I care about stability *and* I care about freedom.

5. Consider the what-ifs and the possibilities related to your decision and write them down too. What-ifs are the things we silently ask or imagine. Possibilities are the different ways we can see this decision playing out or different answers we can imagine for our question right now.

The things written below the waterline appear in various chapters of this book, so, as you or your group take this journey, you will be guided in how to address everything that's been listed.

CHAPTER 2: SURRENDERING

Whenever you are feeling worried, stuck, or powerless, use the surrendering exercise to center yourself.

1. Choose one of these surrender postures:
   - Lying on your stomach with your forehead against your folded hands.
   - Lying on your back with your arms out to your side.
   - Sitting childlike with your feet under your bum and your palms out in front of you.
   - Sitting in a chair or your wheelchair with your palms out in front of you.

- Assuming a different surrender posture that is good for your body.

2. Refer to the iceberg that you drew in chapter 1 and offer everything on it—everything above and below the waterline—to God. Relinquish your feelings, past difficulties, contending convictions and values, what-ifs, and possibilities.

3. Accept what is. Acknowledge the state of your circumstances. Be honest. Allow what is to just be without trying to change it right now.

4. Surrender. Render what you are dealing with to God. Submit it for investigation.

Rest in your surrender posture for five minutes or more—as long as it takes to slow your breathing and heart rate. Return to the surrender exercise as often as you need to.

CHAPTER 3: SEEKING

Use the listening exercise to invite a group of people to assist you in processing a decision and its various possibilities and pathways by asking questions, praying, and providing feedback and wisdom.

The listening exercise can be done in person or online. You can either invite a group of people to help you or you can bring a group together that has several members with a decision to process and everyone can help one another. If multiple people are trying to make the decision, go through the process below one person at a time. You may need to meet a few different times to help multiple people.

1. Explain the decision and the struggle.

2. Spend five to ten minutes in silence.

3. Have the members of the group ask questions to the person who is trying to figure out what to do.

4. The members of the group should focus on asking capacious, curious questions rather than on providing answers.

5. After twenty to thirty minutes of questions, group members can pray together.

6.   After prayer time, group members can share any images or words that came to them during question or prayer time.

The listening exercise will help you to fill out the chart that's related to the searching chapter in this appendix. You can do this exercise with a few different groups in order to consider new ideas and name possibilities and pathways.

CHAPTER 4: SENSING

Use the six E's of emotion exercise to express your emotions in a constructive way.

E-motion: Where are you feeling an emotion in your body? Release this energy by grunting, humming, taking deep breaths in and long breaths out. Or go on a stroll or move to music.

Exact: Use the Internet to search for a feelings wheel. There are many types you can view. They are colorful circles with multiple kinds of feelings written in sections all over the wheel. Look at the middle of the image and figure out the general type of feeling that you are experiencing: mad, sad, happy, etc., and then work outward from the middle to discover exactly what kind of meaning you are making of your emotions and thus what you are feeling.

Express: Tell God what you are feeling. God listens to you and cares about what you are experiencing. Ask God to help you explore, evaluate, and examine your feelings.

Explore: As best you can, be an investigator and an observer. Picture the activating events in your mind. Imagine yourself as a fly on the wall seeing it all play out. Articulate to yourself what happened. When did this feeling begin? What triggered it?

Evaluate: Is there another way to look at what is happening, another way to tell the story? What is the most helpful or charitable way to think about the story or respond to it? Should you reach out to someone else and get a different perspective? Is this related to something that *just* happened or to a past event? Are you experiencing the present through the past? Can the story be reframed? If not, simply move on to the next E, examine.

Examine: What insight can you gain?

Does something need to change?

Do you need something you can give yourself—rest; sleep; unplugging from texting, email, news, and social media platforms; exercise; a reset; a boundary; to say no?

Do you need to limit a substance that is causing your emotions to fluctuate: sugar, alcohol, other substances?

Do you need to articulate a want or need to someone else in a clear, kind way—an apology, equity, love, gentleness, patience, different communication, affirmation, something else?

Do you need to talk to a friend or therapist about what happened?

Do you need to work through your past?

Now that you've worked through your emotion, you have more of an understanding of your current circumstances and what to do next.

CHAPTER 5: SUMMONING

The "museum of your life" exercise helps you to remember who you are.

Imagine that your life has been put into a museum with five rooms. Each room contains memorabilia or interesting art that represents you. If you like, after each time you close your eyes to imagine the room, you can also write down what you saw.

One room has a bunch of pedestals with objects that represent the times in life that your heart was broken. What do you see? Close your eyes and give yourself time to imagine walking through this room and picking up these artifacts. These artifacts represent what and who matters most to you.

Another room has a slide show of the moments you have felt most alive, most free. What moments would the slide show share? Close your eyes and give yourself time to imagine this slide show. This slide show provides insight into the things that nourish your life.

In the next room, the walls have wallpaper with the instances in your life that have filled you with joy. Close your eyes and give yourself time to imagine moments in your life that have been full of meaning, goodness, connection, and living truthfully. This room helps you to determine the things that renew you and fill your heart with purpose.

Another room has framed photos of times you have felt deeply loved—by others, by God, by you. Close your eyes and give yourself time to imagine moments like this. The photos in this room reveal what comforts and heals you.

The last room has paintings of the instants in your life that you have been at peace and felt whole. Even if this room has only a few moments captured, close your eyes and take some time to imagine these as large murals. This is the room that shows us what helps us to feel undivided and in harmony with ourselves, others, creation, and God.

This museum of your life tells you a lot about the stories that you have lived and what makes you, you. It helps you to imagine a hopeful future you can live toward in light of some of the most important aspects of your life.

CHAPTER 6: SHEDDING

The shedding exercise creates the conditions for something new to come forth.

Take some time to reflect. Is there anything you need to shed?

Do you need to forgive someone else, forgive yourself, shed a part of your story or a previous version of yourself? Do you need to shed a relationship or a pattern, or perhaps something good that is no longer good for your life? Do you need to shed a vision?

If you can think of something or a few somethings you would like to subtract from your life, I invite you to talk with God about finding the strength, courage, and help you need to do this.

Now, think through what it will take. What is your plan? Do you need someone else's help? Do you need a book or podcast or app to give you some guidance? Do you need to talk with a therapist, spiritual director, pastor, or counselor? Do you need something else?

Once you have decided what to shed, consider doing something concrete to represent what you are doing.

- You could write a letter to yourself about what you are shedding, why, and how, and then burn the letter safely outside.
- You could find a rock and write a word on it that represents what you are shedding and throw it into a nearby body of water.

Allow the memory of whatever you do to give you strength to keep moving forward.

Anytime you are feeling weighed down by the past, you can use the shedding exercise to help you keep moving forward.

CHAPTER 7: SIFTING

The sifting beliefs exercise is helpful when you are wrestling with what to believe.

Describe the beliefs that you have held that are being challenged. You can write them down or draw them or write poetry or music or talk with a friend about them. Reflect on the origins of each belief and what is at stake for you or the community regarding each belief. Do you need to gather more information?

Chapter 7 describes three options. There are others, but perhaps one below is resonating with you as you consider your contending convictions.

Rejection: Is it time to release an old belief and embrace a new one in its place (and enter into a very intentional healing process)? There are ideas for shaping a healing process in chapter 10.

Expansion: Have you had an illumination that has sharpened your perspective and thus deepened, expanded, or added to what you already knew?

Paradox: Have you been holding on to two beliefs, trying to choose between them, only to realize you can add the word "and" so both are true and you can actually continue to believe both?

Consider having a conversation with someone you trust in order to verbally process your beliefs and how this exercise impacts your decision-making process.

CHAPTER 8: SELECTING

The values exercise helps you to clearly articulate your values so that you can make decisions that are in line with what matters most to God, the communities you care about, and you.

Spiritual values: love, joy, peace, patience, kindness, goodness, gentleness, faithfulness, self-control, mercy, justice, compassion, shalom, wholeness, redemption, restoration, healing.

(Scriptures to read for reflecting on Christian spiritual values: Psalm 85; Isaiah 26; Matthew 21:12–17; Luke 15; Luke 7; Romans 8:31–39; Galatians 5:22–23; Philippians 4.)

Add to the list in light of the Scriptures and stories you know about God.

- List one, two, or three spiritual values that are connected to the decision you are trying to make. What kinds of actions will help you to nurture these values?

    Common core values: acceptance, achievement, adventure, advocacy, authenticity, balance, belonging, community, consistency, collaboration, courage, creativity, duty, encouragement, ethics, empathy, equity, excellence, fairness, family, friendship, flexibility, freedom, fun, gain, generosity, growth, health, honesty, humility, humor, independence, integrity, insight, intuition, joy, kindness, knowledge, legacy, loyalty, making a difference, mindfulness, motivation, open-mindedness, optimism, power, recognition, resilience, resourcefulness, responsibility, safety, security, selflessness, stability, success, teamwork, thankfulness, traditionalism, trustworthiness, understanding, vision, wealth, well-being, wisdom, zeal.

- Review the list of common core values and choose three values in light of your decision that deeply matter in the communities that are important to you (family, friends, church/religious community, workplace, neighborhood, organizations you frequent).
- Review the list of common core values and choose three values in light of your decision that deeply matter to you.
- As you look at the lists you made of spiritual values, communal values, and personal values, what do you notice? And what comes up for you?
- How might one or more of these values guide your decision-making process?

Return to the values exercise whenever you're trying to figure out what matters most in relation to a particular decision.

CHAPTER 9: SEARCHING

Use the charting exercise to figure out what you know and don't know so you can discern what to do next in any decision-making process.

Draw a 4-inch by 4-inch square on a big piece of paper with four boxes, two columns and two rows. Label the columns "Known" and "Unknown" and the rows "Known" and "Unknown." This is known as the Rumsfeld quadrant, or the Johari Window.

- In the first square, "known knowns," write down the variables and facts that you are aware of that you know regarding your decision. For example, you may know what percentage of money you would give up or a value that you could more wholeheartedly live if you took a certain path.

- In the next box, "known unknowns," write variables, questions, or factors that are gaps in your knowledge. For example, you may know you feel scared, but you're not sure why. Is there a possibility you need to learn more about? Can you break this box up into a few smaller decisions? What do you need to learn more about to feel comfortable making this decision?

- The next box is "unknown knowns," and these are the identified risks and challenges. You might talk with others who have gone through something similar or with those who counsel people in making your kind of decision, or you might even talk with people who have a stake in your decision.

- The final box is "unknown unknowns," those things we are not aware of and do not understand. These are the unidentified risks. Can you think of potential surprises or unforeseen consequences or implications of your decision? Can you or people you trust come up with any? Even if this is blank, this is all right. It is important just to acknowledge that there are some things that you have yet to know that you do not know.

Filling out these boxes shows you that decision making is not about prediction, but prudence. We can carefully consider each of the boxes and do our research; take these things to God; talk these things over with trusted companions; consider various pathways; and reflect on how we might navigate potential problems or roadblocks. But we cannot know everything. And that's okay. No one can. You can simply try to make the best decision possible with what you know and can learn about.

CHAPTER 10: STRIVING

Use the "highlight reel" exercise whenever you need inspiration.

Take a stroll, grab a journal, or sit with someone who loves you and consider the questions below in light of the highlight reel of your life—the major events, the incredible highs, the nearly unspeakable lows.

- When you consider the story you've lived so far, what comes up for you?
- When you think about change, what happens in your body? Describe it. Why do you think this is?
- When you think about what is happening right now in your life—the decision, the shift, the possible change, the question—in the context of the highlight reel of your life, what stands out to you? Have you been here before? What connections between the past and the present can you make?
- What have you overcome? When has your strength shown up?

Thinking about where we've been can motivate us to keep moving forward.

CHAPTER 11: SATED JOY

This gratitude practice is designed to be done after your decision. This gratitude practice will help you to see what has emerged and how this journey has transformed you. It can be done alone or with others. Find somewhere meaningful to you to do this practice. I am going to provide some prompts. You can write them out in your journal or say them like a prayer. If you're with someone else, you can have a conversation about them.

- Reflect on what this decision-making process has taught you. Thank God, yourself, and others for all that you have learned.
- Meditate on the people who have supported you during your decision-making process. Allow the moments they helped you, encouraged you, and lifted you up to come into your mind. Visualize each one. Express thanks for these people and these moments.
- Consider the times that God spoke to you during this process—through others, dreams, synchronicity, signs, nature, your inner knowing, confirmation. Give thanks to God.
- Think about the inner work you have done. Describe what you

have done to participate in your own healing. Thank God and yourself for this restorative work.

- Imagine the future. Picture yourself expressing sated joy. What do you look like? Where are you? Are you with others, and if so, who? Give thanks to God for what is to come.

This gratitude practice helps you to live toward your new story.

GRATITUDE

To the incredible humans who helped me make the two most difficult decisions of my life, family, friends, colleagues, mentors:

Dear sisters Stef Poulin, Alli Williams, Jenna Olney, who took me in and sat with me for hours and reassured me. I love you. Jenna, I remember the day in Ro's room by his crib like it was yesterday. Thank you.

To my amazing mom, Jenny Douglas, and my wonderful bonus dad, Don Douglas, what would I do without your audacious love? Thank you for forever being in my corner. And for selling my books wherever you go! I can come to you and ask for anything I need. What a gift. I love you both to the moon and back.

To my extended family, thank you for your enduring love and encouragement. To my aunt Delena, thanks for Christmas 2020. I won't ever forget how you helped me.

To Molly Galbraith, for that week in October and all those times you've said yes to having me visit. For every loving reminder that I am capable, for every way you have invested in me and loved me. To Sarah Mosher, for the driveway conversations and the party, and to Jake Student and the rest of your awesome family for our weekly dinners after my divorce. They meant the world to me. I'll never get over them. To Mary Alice Birdwhistell, for every time you asked me incredible questions and listened so attentively, allowing me to be my truest, most authentic self with you. To Macy Workman, for your care packages and texts and calls that have always gotten me through.

To Chris Kelby Powell, thanks for companioning with me as I wrote this entire book. For truly seeing me and all you have taught me. For August 2022 and the countless other ways you've showed up for me. I am incredibly grateful for you.

To Michaela O'Donnell Long, for taking every frantic call during the hardest time of my life and asking all the right questions. To Beth Chiaravalle, for that gathering that rescued me and for making me feel like no matter what I chose that I would be okay. To Lyndsey Deane Ratchford, for that lunch in 2013 and every other meal since that has given me strength. To Liz Kronenberg, for letting me stay at your LA apartment and the numerous times you processed with me and encouraged me. To Anne Jeffrey and Devan Stahl, for crying with me and being so trustworthy and so wildly supportive at every turn. To Chloe James, for your cooking and love that has sustained me.

To Joy Moton, graduate assistant turned colleague and friend, for all of the ways you supported me while my life was falling apart. For your enduring kindness and love. To Casey Sasek for your kitchen conversations that inspired me and made me believe in myself. To Drew Collins for your endless cheering me on, and to Justin Crisp for your enlightening questions.

Much gratitude to giants of the faith Willie James Jennings and Parker Palmer too. Your time is so precious and you are so wise.

I hold the conversations I had with every one of you in my heart. I remember your words and your wisdom. I remember the various ways each of you made time for me, held space with me. You lifted me up. *When I think of people who have loved me back to life, I think of you.* From the bottom of my heart, thank you.

To my former students at Baylor who took my courses and helped me to workshop these ideas, thank you so much. I am especially grateful for the discernment group who came to my living room in spring 2022. Thanks for praying, dreaming, and listening to God together. You know who you are.

To my former colleagues who journeyed with me in my difficult decisions, thank you for your compassion and understanding. That last dinner lives in me. And thanks for our office and hallway chats and for our lunches and the good times before graduations! And for all of you who have texted, emailed, and called me since leaving, I'm so thankful.

For the people who made this book possible:

To Christian Peele and her trusted friends, your list of heroes and sheroes throughout history was incredibly helpful and inspiring for me. Thank you. For other friends and colleagues who helped me think about people to study for this book and for our conversations about it, especially David Wilhite, Ryan McAnnally-Linz, Ryan Ramsey. I appreciate you!

Multiple people said yes to being interviewed for this book. For the sake of privacy, I will not list everyone, but you know who you are. Thank you so much for sharing some of the most important decisions of your life with me and trusting me with your stories.

Many people responded on social media to my posts and stories as I was doing research for this book. I am so grateful for your vulnerable replies, your examples, and your questions. It helped me immensely.

To the incredible team at Faith+Lead and the Glorify app, thank you for letting me workshop ideas for this book and share what I learned while writing it with your great people.

Lisa Ann Cockrel, from the first time we met for dinner in cold Grand Rapids, I knew we would be friends! Thanks for championing this book. You are incredibly creative and wise. I have so much gratitude for the ways you inspired me to edit this book and for your careful attention to every line. Huge thanks to the whole team at Eerdmans for all of your amazing work!

To my book agents, Laura Bardolph and David Bratt of BBH Literary, what would I do without you! Thank you for our meaningful conversations about navigating difficult decisions. And for our many dinners and text threads. When I think of the people who nurture the light within and help people to keep moving forward, I think of both of you. You are wildly loving, thoughtful, and courageous. For everything, thank you.

NOTES

13 "SOME THINGS BREAK" Billie Eidson Music, accessed March 17, 2024, https://www.billieeidsonmusic.com/must-read/some -things-break-our-hearts-but-fix-our-vision.

15 TRUST THE PROCESS Max Rappaport, "The Definitive History of 'Trust the Process,'" *Bleacher Report*, August 23, 2017, https:// bleacherreport.com/articles/2729018-the-definitive-history-of -trust-the-process.

15 SCHOLAR ELAINE JAMES Elaine James, "A Word to the Wise," Princeton Theological Seminary Convocation, September 15, 2022, https://www.youtube.com/watch?v=AnvIJVotYU4.

16 "LOOK WELL TO" Howard Thurman, *The Growing Edge* (New York: Harper, 1956), front matter.

19 IÑIGO DE LOYOLA WAS BORN Ludwig Marcuse, *Soldier of the Church: The Life of St. Ignatius of Loyola*, ed. and trans. Christopher Lazare (New York: Simon & Schuster, 1939), 31–41; "The Life of St. Ignatius of Loyola," Jesuits, accessed May 14, 2024, https://www.jesuits .org/stories/the-life-of-st-ignatius-of-loyola/.

20 THERE, HE SURRENDERED HIS SWORD Anthony Lilles, "Montserrat and St. Ignatius," Beginning to Pray, accessed May 14, 2024, https://beginningtopray.blogspot.com/2011/08/montserrat-and -stignatius.html.

24 OF ALL OF THE INTERVIEWS   Lydia, phone interview by Angela Williams Gorrell, April 25, 2023.

26 SURRENDER IS AN   Cynthia Bourgeault, *The Wisdom Way of Knowing: Reclaiming an Ancient Tradition to Awaken the Heart* (San Francisco: Jossey-Bass, 2003), 72.

27 "BY GETTING LOST AND WELCOMING"   Cameron Trimble, "In Times of Turbulence, Fly Loose," *Oneing* 11, no. 1, *Transitions* (Spring 2023): 32, 35–36, 37.

27 "FAITH, ON THE OTHER HAND"   Alan W. Watts, *The Wisdom of Insecurity: A Message for an Age of Anxiety* (New York: Vintage Books, 1951, 1968), 24.

28 "INTERIOR SURRENDER IS OFTEN"   Bourgeault, *The Wisdom Way*, 75.

35 "LADY WISDOM GOES"   Prov. 9:3–6 The Message.

35 THE QUAKER RELIGIOUS   "Clearness Committees," FGC Friends General Convention, accessed May 14, 2024, https://www.fgc quaker.org/fgcresources/practical/practices/clearness-commit tees/. For an example of how a clearness committee helped him make a big decision, see Parker Palmer, *Let Your Life Speak: Listening for the Voice of Vocation* (San Francisco: Jossey-Bass, 2000), 44–46.

36 SPECIFICALLY,   Frederick Douglass, *My Bondage and My Freedom* (1855; reprint, New York: Penguin Books, 2003), 605.

36 "THE READING OF THESE SPEECHES"   Douglass, *My Bondage and My Freedom*, 533.

36 "PENDING THE TIME OF OUR CONTEMPLATED"   Douglass, *My Bondage and My Freedom*, 608.

37   "WE WERE, AT TIMES, CONFIDENT"   Douglass, *My Bondage and My Freedom*, 609.

38   IT'S WISE TO TALK   Mary C. Earle, *The Desert Mothers: Spiritual Practices from the Women of the Wilderness* (Harrisburg, NY: Morehouse Publishing, 2007), 43.

38   "WHAT WOULD YOU"   Justin Crisp, questions for discernment, in-person conversation, June 2022.

39   IT IS EASY FOR   Author and public theologian Brian McLaren describes how bias works in how we see things and make decisions during season 2 of his podcast, *Learning How to See*, https://cac.org/podcast/learning-how-to-see/?season=lhts-two#season-details.

39   "SECRETS MAKE YOU SICK"   Marcus Zoom, interviewed by Angela Williams Gorrell, April 13, 2023.

44   DURING OUR PHONE INTERVIEW   Carol, phone interview by Angela Williams Gorrell, April 10, 2023.

45   AS GOD DID FOR CAROL   Henri Nouwen calls people "living signs." Henri Nouwen, *Discernment: Reading the Signs of Daily Life* (New York: HarperOne, 2013), 63.

47   IT MAY SURPRISE YOU   Maxwell King, *The Good Neighbor: The Life and Work of Fred Rogers* (New York: Abrams, 2018).

48   "THIS WAS A PIVOTAL THEME"   King, *The Good Neighbor*, 3: College Days.

48   "FRED ROGERS TOOK PROFOUND"   King, *The Good Neighbor*, 3.

49   WE CAN'T CHOOSE BETWEEN   Antonio R. Damasio, "We Feel, Therefore We Learn; The Relevance of Affective and Social Neuroscience to Education," and Kurt W. Fischer, "Neuroscience Bases of

Learning," both in *Emotions, Learning, and the Brain: Exploring the Educational Implications of Affective Neuroscience*, ed. Mary Helen Immordino-Yang (New York: Norton, 2015).

49 YOUR FEELINGS ARE ALSO INTEGRAL Damasio, "We Feel, Therefore We Learn," and Fischer, "Neuroscience Bases of Learning."

50 YOUR FEELINGS ARE IMPORTANT Damasio, "We Feel, Therefore We Learn," and Fischer, "Neuroscience Bases of Learning."

50 THE FEELING OF WONDER Ulrich Weger and Johannes Wagemann, "Towards a Conceptual Clarification of Awe and Wonder: A First Person Phenomenological Inquiry," *Current Psychology: A Journal for Diverse Perspectives on Diverse Psychological Issues* 40, no. 3 (2021): 1386–1401.

50 "WONDER FUELS OUR PASSION" Brené Brown, *Atlas of the Heart: Mapping Meaningful Connection and the Language of Human Experience* (New York: Random House, 2021), 59.

50 CURIOSITY AND INTEREST George Loewenstein, "The Psychology of Curiosity: A Review and Reinterpretation," *Psychological Bulletin* 116, no. 1 (1994): 94.

51 AWE IS ANOTHER HELPFUL FEELING Dacher Keltner and Jonathan Haidt, "Approaching Awe, a Moral, Spiritual, and Aesthetic Emotion," *Cognition and Emotion* 17, no. 2 (2003): 297–314, 312.

52 E-MOTION: EMOTIONS ARE "ENERGY IN MOTION," Dr. Frida Rundell, Zoom meeting, March 29, 2023.

52 EXACT: DO YOUR BEST TO CATEGORIZE Lisa Feldman Barrett, *How Emotions Are Made: The Secret Life of the Brain* (reprint, New York: Harper Paperbacks, 2018), 205. Feldman calls this "higher emotional granularity," 182.

53 EVALUATE: IS THERE ANOTHER WAY Barrett, *How Emotions Are Made*, 197.

59 EXPRESS: GOD TRULY CARES ABOUT Angela Williams Gorrell, *The Gravity of Joy: A Story of Being Lost and Found* (Grand Rapids: Eerdmans, 2021), 124.

59 LAMENTS ARE ADDRESSED "Lamentations," Bible Project, accessed May 15, 2024, https://bibleproject.com/explore/video/lamen tations/.

60 LAMENT DRAWS ATTENTION TO INJUSTICE "Habakkuk," Bible Project, accessed May 15, 2024, https://bibleproject.com/explore/video /habakkuk/.

62 "FEAR IS AN ENERGY" John Chryssavgis, *In the Heart of the Desert: The Spirituality of the Desert Fathers and Mothers* (Bloomington, IN: World Wisdom, 2003), 107.

65 AS SHE TRIED TO TEACH Marlene Targ Brill, *Dolores Huerta Stands Strong: The Woman Who Demanded Justice* (Athens: Ohio University Press, 2018); *Dolores*, directed by Peter Bratt (Carlos Santana Production, 2017), 1 hour 35 minutes, https://www.doloresthe movie.com.

67 "I WAS ENTRUSTED WITH CARRYING VOICES" Joy Harjo, *Crazy Brave: A Memoir* (New York: Norton, 2012), 20.

67 "CÉSAR CHAVEZ AND MY MOTHER" *Dolores*, directed by Peter Bratt.

68 "WE HAVE A TENDENCY" *Dolores*, directed by Peter Bratt.

68 DOLORES'S GRANDFATHER WATCHED HER Brill, *Dolores Huerta Stands Strong*, 10.

69 "THIS IS MY LIFE'S WORK" *Dolores*, directed by Peter Bratt.

72 AS MY FRIEND PATRICK I learned about the power of visualizing people who have loved us through theologian, educator, and writer Patrick B. Reyes, who was taught this practice by his beloved grandma. He asks, "Who has loved you into being?" in his book *The Purpose Gap: Empowering Communities of Color to Find Meaning and Thrive* (Louisville: Westminster John Knox, 2021), 43.

72   SIMILARLY, WHEN I WAS TRYING   John Berardi, *Changemaker: Turn Your Passion for Health and Fitness into a Powerful Purpose and Wildly Successful Career* (Dallas: BenBella Books, 2019), 40.

73   "WE ARE LED TO TRUTH"   Parker Palmer, *Let Your Life Speak: Listening for the Voice of Vocation* (San Francisco: Jossey-Bass, 2000), 22.

74   MARY MCLEOD BETHUNE WAS   Nancy Ann Zrinyi Long, *Mary McLeod Bethune: Her Life and Legacy* (Cocoa, FL: Florida Historical Society Press, 2019).

76   HERE IS AN IMPORTANT STORY   Gen. 1. I am endorsing the view of original blessing. Jonathan Merritt, "Author: Jesus Didn't Believe in 'Original Sin' and Neither Should We," Religion News Service, January 13, 2017, https://religionnews.com/2017/01/13/author -jesus-didnt-believe-in-original-sin-and-neither-should-we/.

76   "YOU LOVE EVERYTHING THAT EXISTS"   Wisdom of Solomon 11:24.

77   LISA MILLER IS A CLINICAL PSYCHOLOGIST   Lisa Miller, *The Awakened Brain: The Psychology of Spirituality* (New York: Penguin, 2022).

81   "WE DON'T GIVE ENOUGH GLORY"   Joy Sullivan, untitled, printed with permission.

82   "RACHEL WAS OUR PASTOR"   Laura Jean Truman, "I'm Here Because of Her: Rachel Held Evans," Laura Jean Truman, May 5, 2019, https://laurajeantruman.com/2019/05/05/im-here-because-of -her-rachel-held-evans/.

82   RACHEL WAS KNOWN   Rachel Held Evans, *Searching for Sunday: Loving, Leaving, and Finding the Church* (Nashville: Nelson, 2015).

82   "ON SUNDAY MORNINGS"   Evans, *Searching for Sunday*, 57.

82   "I WAS SURROUNDED BY"   Evans, *Searching for Sunday*, 58.

83   "I PUT MY HEAD IN MY HANDS"   Evans, *Searching for Sunday*, 65.

83   THROUGHOUT   Evans, *Searching for Sunday*, xviii.

83   THE SPIRITUAL LIFE   Meister Eckhart, "Sermon on the Fourth Sunday after Trinity," in *Meister Eckhart: Selected Treatises and Sermons*, translated from Latin and German with an introduction and notes, trans. James M. Clark and John V. Skinner (London: Faber & Faber, 1958), 194.

84   JESUS GAVE US A PROFOUND   John 15.

84   SOMETIMES WE NEED TO   Comment on how sometimes we need to break on the way to wholeness is from Maggie Smith, *Keep Moving: Notes on Loss, Creativity, Change* (New York: Atria/One Signal Publishers, 2020).

84   "WHEN WE LEARN WHAT TO LET GO OF"   John Chryssavgis, *In the Heart of the Desert: The Spirituality of the Desert Fathers and Mothers* (Bloomington, IN: World Wisdom, 2003), 69.

84   "FORGIVENESS IS A PROCESS"   Miroslav Volf, "Consider Forgiveness," YouTube, accessed May 15, 2024, https://www.youtube.com/watch?v=x8fbjzQcTws.

84   FORGIVENESS IS AKIN TO   Robert Enright, "The Power of Forgiveness," PBS, May 13, 2008, https://www.pbs.org/video/university-place-the-power-of-forgiveness-ep-162/.

85   FORGIVENESS IS YOUR GIFT   Miroslav Volf, *Free of Charge: Giv-*

ing and Forgiving in a Culture Stripped of Grace (Grand Rapids: Zondervan, 2006).

86   SEVERAL YEARS EARLIER   William, phone interview by Angela Williams Gorrell, April 13, 2023.

86   MANY PEOPLE WHO FACE   Chad M. S. Steel et al., "Suicidal Ideation in Offenders Convicted of Child Sexual Exploitation Material Offences," *Behavioral Sciences and the Law* 40, no. 3 (May/June 2022): 365–78, doi: 10.1002/bsl.2560.

86   "THE SPIRITUAL LIFE IS A STRUGGLE"   Mary C. Earle, *The Desert Mothers: Spiritual Practices from the Women of the Wilderness* (Harrisburg, NY: Morehouse Publishing, 2007), 51.

87   THE APOSTLE PAUL WAS WALKING   Acts 9.

91   "YOU CAN HAVE COMPASSION"   Amanda E. White, Instagram post, December 6, 2020.

92   ONE OF THE MOST SIGNIFICANT   Melody Beattie, *Codependent No More: How to Stop Controlling Others and Start Caring for Yourself* (Spiegel & Grau by OrangeSky Audio, 2022), chapter 5.

94   MORGAN HARPER NICHOLS   Morgan Harper Nichols poem, Instagram post, November 21, 2020.

95   ANNE HUTCHINSON HAD A DYNAMIC   Emery John Battis, *Saints and Sectaries: Anne Hutchinson and the Antinomian Controversy in the Massachusetts Bay Colony* (Chapel Hill: University of North Carolina Press, 1962), 6.

95   "HAD SHE BEEN BORN INTO"   Battis, *Saints and Sectaries*, 6.

98   AS I INTERVIEWED GEN   Gen, phone interview by Angela Williams Gorrell, April 10, 2023.

102 JESSE WAS ALSO WILLING TO BE INTERVIEWED Jesse, phone interview by Angela Williams Gorrell, April 24, 2023.

105 WHEN I INTERVIEWED ROSELINE Roseline, phone interview by Angela Williams Gorrell, April 25, 2023.

107 PERHAPS THE COGNITIVE DISSONANCE Molly Galbraith, phone conversation, May 12, 2023.

109 AMMA SYNCLETICA WAS Mary C. Earle, *The Desert Mothers: Spiritual Practices from the Women of the Wilderness* (Harrisburg, NY: Morehouse Publishing, 2007), 29–30.

110 "WHAT GOOD WILL IT BE" Matt. 16:26 NIV.

110 AFTER A LONG TIME Mariel Mastrostefano, "A Desert Mother: Amma Syncletica," CBE International, March 7, 2012, https://www.cbeinternational.org/resource/desert-mother-amma-syncletica/.

113 THE PAIN OF MY THIRTIES Angela Williams Gorrell, *The Gravity of Joy: A Story of Being Lost and Found* (Grand Rapids: Eerdmans, 2021).

114 CENTURIES AFTER AMMA AND HER SISTER, JOHN AND VERA MAE PERKINS Stephen E. Berk, *A Time to Heal: John Perkins, Community Development, and Racial Reconciliation* (Grand Rapids: Baker Books, 1997).

115 "AS JOHN THOUGHT ABOUT THE ALTERNATIVE" Berk, *A Time to Heal*, 76.

117 "I MUST LISTEN TO MY LIFE" Parker Palmer, *Let Your Life Speak: Listening for the Voice of Vocation* (San Francisco: Jossey-Bass, 2000), 4–5.

117 THEY DID MINISTRY THROUGH COMMUNITY DEVELOPMENT "Our History," John and Vera Mae Perkins Foundation, accessed May 17, 2024, https://www.jvmpf.org/our-history/.

119 AS AN EXTRAORDINARY COMPETITOR Jackie Robinson, *I Never Had It Made: An Autobiography* (New York: HarperCollins, 1995).

120   "HE HAD TO BE ABLE TO STAND UP"   Robinson, *I Never Had It Made*, 28.

120   "PLENTY OF TIMES I WANTED"   This is one of Jackie Robinson's most famous quotes, and it is difficult to know the exact time and place he first said it. Houston Mitchell, "Dodgers Dugout: Jackie Robinson Deserves More Than Just a Day," *Los Angeles Times*, April 15, 2021, https://www.latimes.com/sports/newsletter/2021-04-15/jackie-robinson-dodgers-dugout.

120   "RACHEL'S UNDERSTANDING LOVE WAS"   Robinson, *I Never Had It Made*, 54.

120   "I REMEMBERED THE THINGS"   Robinson, *I Never Had It Made*, 41.

121   "GOD GIVES HIS BEST"   Matt. 5:45 The Message.

123   "THE FEAR OF LOSS"   Joan Chittister, *Between the Darkness and the Daylight* (Chadstone, Australia: Images Publishing, 2015), 38.

123   "CERTAINTY, FOR ALL OF ITS GUARANTEES"   Chittister, *Between the Darkness and the Daylight*, 40.

124   "DON'T ASK WHAT THE WORLD"   The history of this quote is muddled. It appeared in a section called "In Gratitude" in a book written by Gil Bailie, who says Thurman said it to him around 1974. *Violence Unveiled: Humanity at the Crossroads* (New York: Crossroad, 1994).

124   "SWEET DARKNESS,"   David Whyte, "Sweet Darkness," in *The House of Belonging* (Vancouver, BC: Many Rivers Press, 1997), 23. It has been quoted many times in many places. For example, David Whyte, "Sweet Darkness," YouTube, July 18, 2021, https://www.youtube.com/watch?v=ZIazVjNPPNk.

126   ANTONY WAS AN EGYPTIAN,   *Athanasius: The Life of Antony and the Letter to Marcellinus*, translation and introduction by Robert C. Gregg (New York: Paulist, 1980), 30–42 and 99, and John Chrys-

savgis, *In the Heart of the Desert: The Spirituality of the Desert Fathers and Mothers* (Bloomington, IN: World Wisdom, 2003), 15.

127   WHAT SEASON IS IT?   Eccles. 3.

129   ARE YOU MOVING TOWARD   Vinita Hampton Wright, "Consolation and Desolation," Ignatian Spirituality, accessed May 17, 2024, https://www.ignatianspirituality.com/consolation-and -desolation-2/.

129   "THERE IS A DEEPER VOICE"   Richard Rohr, "Listening to the Voice of God," Center for Action and Contemplation, July 29, 2022, https://cac.org/daily-meditations/listening-to-the-voice-of-god -2022-07-29/.

129   IN THIS STATE OF MOVING   Wright, "Consolation and Desolation." This web page also integrates ideas from the work of author and spiritual director Margaret Silf.

129   "THE SCRIPTURES TELL US"   Shane Claiborne, Jonathan Wilson-Hartgrove, and Enuma Okoro, *Common Prayer: A Liturgy for Ordinary Radicals* (Grand Rapids: Zondervan, 2010), 176.

130   JESUS'S ENCOUNTER WITH ZACCHAEUS   Luke 19:1–9 NIV.

130   THE OTHER STORY IS ABOUT A WOMAN   Luke 8:43–48.

131   A RICH MAN COMES UP TO JESUS   Matt. 19:16–22.

131   ANOTHER FORM OF FILTERING   Elizabeth Liebert, *The Way of Discernment: Spiritual Practices for Decision Making* (Louisville: Westminster John Knox, 2008), 96. For information on the helpfulness of mental practice, see "Mental Practice: What It Is and How to Use It," *Effectiviology,* accessed May 17, 2024, https://effectiviology .com/the-power-of-mental-practice/. For the study of golfers, see Cornelia Frank et al., "Mental Representation and Mental Practice:

Experimental Investigation on the Functional Links between Motor Memory and Motor Imagery," *PLOS ONE* 9, no. 4 (April 2014), https://doi.org/10.1371/journal.pone.0095175.

133   "THOUGH I WAS BLURRED"   Joy Harjo, *Crazy Brave: A Memoir* (New York: Norton, 2012), 81.

134   AS JOY HELD THIS BROCHURE   Harjo, *Crazy Brave*, 82.

134   GIDEON DID THIS   Judg. 6:36–40.

137   PETER BUXTUN WAS TWENTY-SEVEN YEARS OLD   Carl Elliot, "Tuskegee Truth Teller: Peter Buxtun, like Many Medical Whistleblowers, Got Little Thanks for Exposing a Notorious Scandal," *American Scholar* 87, no. 1 (2018).

137   THE PARTICIPANTS HAD NO IDEA   Derek Kerr and Maria Rivero, "Whistleblower Peter Buxtun and the Tuskegee Syphilis Study," Government Accountability Project, April 30, 2014, https://whis tleblower.org/uncategorized/whistleblower-peter-buxtun-and-the -tuskegee-syphilis-study/.

138   "WHEN THEY COME TO FIRE YOU"   Elliot, "Tuskegee Truth Teller," 48.

141   HERE ARE A FEW OF THE MANY GOOD REASONS   Nedra Tawwab, Instagram post, December 15, 2021. For more on her and her work, see www.nedratawwab.com.

146   READ ABOUT REAL SELF-CARE   Pooja Lakshmin, *Real Self-Care: A Transformative Program for Redefining Wellness* (London: Penguin Life, 2023).

147   ANNA MAY WONG   Katie Gee Salisbury, *Not Your China Doll* (New York: Penguin Random House, 2024), xii.

147   "SHE INTRODUCED THE AMERICAN PUBLIC" Salisbury, *Not Your China Doll*, xii.

147   WHILE GROWING UP Salisbury, *Not Your China Doll*, 5.

147   "HIT THE CEILING" Salisbury, *Not Your China Doll*, 39.

147   "IF YOU LET ME PLAY" Salisbury, *Not Your China Doll*, 256.

147   "ANNA MAY GOT TO THINKING" Salisbury, *Not Your China Doll*, 310.

148   "THE VERY SAME COINS" Salisbury, *Not Your China Doll*, 383.

150   PERPETUA JOURNALED Vibia Perpetua, *The Passion of Perpetua and Felicity*, trans. Thomas J. Heffernan (Oxford: Oxford University Press, 2012), 125–35. On Perpetua's journal, see Joyce Ellen Salisbury, "Perpetua," *Britannica*, last updated April 24, 2024, https://www.britannica.com/biography/Perpetua-Christian-martyr.

151   AS MICHAELA O'DONNELL LONG Long pointed out that most of us prefer chronic pain over acute pain during a conversation. It has stayed with me ever since.

151   DOROTHY DAY KNOWS ABOUT Dorothy Day, *The Long Loneliness: The Autobiography of Dorothy Day* (San Francisco: Harper & Row, 1952). For Day and the Catholic Worker Movement, see Casey Cep, "Dorothy Day's Radical Faith," *New Yorker*, April 6, 2020, https://www.newyorker.com/magazine/2020/04/13/dorothy-days-radical-faith.

151   "EVEN BEFORE THE GREAT DEPRESSION" Cep, "Dorothy Day's Radical Faith."

152   "I WANTED TO DIE" Day, *The Long Loneliness*, 149.

152   "I NEVER REGRETTED" Day, *The Long Loneliness*, 151.

152 "WHERE DO PEOPLE FIND" Parker Palmer, *Let Your Life Speak: Listening for the Voice of Vocation* (San Francisco: Jossey-Bass, 2000), 34.

153 RATHER, IT ALL MIRACULOUSLY Rom. 8:28.

156 "MARY IS THE MODEL" Richard Rohr, "Saying Yes to Body and Spirit," Center for Action and Contemplation, December 18, 2023, https://cac.org/daily-meditations/saying-yes-to-body-and-spirit/.

157 YOUR HEART ISN'T BROKEN Maggie Smith, *Keep Moving: Notes on Loss, Creativity, and Change* (New York: Atria/One Signal Publishers, 2020).

157 WINESKINS WERE MADE Mark 2:21–22.

159 "LETTING GO HAS CONSEQUENCES" Barbara A. Holmes, *Crisis Contemplation: Healing the Wounded Village* (Albuquerque, NM: CAC Publishing, 2021), 47.

162 "FILLED A DYING MAN'S DAYS" Paul Kalanithi, *When Breath Becomes Air* (London: Random House, 2016), 199.